Hiring Winners

Profile

Interview

Evaluate

A 3-Step
Formula for
Success

Richard J. Pinsker

amacom

American Management Association

Library of Congress Cataloging-in-Publication Data

Pinsker, Richard J.
    Hiring winners : profile, interview, evaluate : a 3-step formula
for success / Richard J. Pinsker.
        p.   cm.
    Includes index.
    ISBN 0-8144-5051-2
    1. Employment interviewing.   2. Employee selection.   I. Title.
HF5549.5.I6P56   1991
658.3'112—dc20   91-23685
                                                                    CIP

Printing number

10 9 8 7 6 5 4 3

In memory of
William and **Bess Pinsker,**
and
Joshua Todd Griffith, Jr.

Contents

Preface

A client of mine wanted to promote a regional sales manager to the position of vice-president of sales, suddenly available because of a transfer. I asked him if he had upgraded the list of performance expectations that we had developed for the position two years earlier, when the former vice-president had been recruited. The company had grown considerably during the past two years, creating a whole new set of opportunities and associated problems. The client admitted that he had not done this, but he went on to say that it was "logical" to promote this person.

As I had also recruited this regional sales manager several years earlier and had kept up with his progress, the decision surprised me. He was a good regional salesperson, but I doubted his promotability.

Nevertheless, my client was in a hurry to fill the vacated position and made the offer in spite of my misgivings.

Unfortunately, the promotion did not work out. As a regional sales manager, the person had only managed his territory; as vice-president, his job was to manage other regional sales managers, a task for which he was unqualified. He lasted six months before being sent back to regional sales where he belonged, and a costly new search was started for a vice-president of sales.

This situation illustrates some of the most common issues in recruiting or promoting employees:

• Little thought is given to the *specific accomplishments* expected of a person being brought into a position. We tend to think first about the candidate, *then* about defining the results to be achieved. In fact, if we defined the results first, we would have a method of comparing candidates and judging their true abilities.

• With time, job requirements change. What may have been required several years ago is almost certainly not the case today. Because business is dynamic, so are the results we need a person to achieve. Executives need to think through what has changed and what is required each time they proceed with a new hire.

• Executives often state that they need the new hire "yesterday," or that they just don't "have the time" to go through all the required hiring steps. In most of these cases, they will continue to spend more time and money "rehiring" for the same position, ending up with less than a winner.

The PIE Selection System discussed in this book is designed to save you time and money. Whether you apply it to promotions within the company or to new hires, it will force you to proceed with forethought and logic. The result: You will *not* make costly mistakes and you *will* hire winners.

Acknowledgments

To all those clients, educators, fellow consultants, business associates, and friends who, perhaps unknowingly, contributed to a part of my career, and thus this book, I give my warmest, wholehearted thanks—thanks for letting me know you, learn from you, and share with you.

To those clients, specifically, who have allowed me to experiment and test the PIE concept within their corporations, thanks for the opportunity. Your experiences and stories, presented in disguise, will help the reader relate to his or her own situations.

To three individuals—Ron Donati, whose critique and comments on my original manuscript encouraged me to continue with this book; Trevor Meldal-Johnsen, whose writing skills helped me translate concepts and experiences to the written word; Adrienne Hickey, my editor at AMACOM, who spared no words in telling me like it was—my gratitude for your help in bringing this book to fruition.

To Jana Heer, whose artistic jacket design so appropriately depicts the "winners," my thanks.

And a special thanks to my lifetime partner and wife, Ginny, for her continued patience and support, and for her putting up with the guy who wakes up at 2 A.M. to write another page.

1

The Hiring Maze

Why hire winners? Because, whether you have only a few employees or thousands, winners make your job easier.

Winners are peak achievers who get more accomplished because they work smarter and harder. Winners require less training, supervision, and motivation. And they save a company money through reduced turnover, better productivity, and decreased recruiting expenses.

The PIE Selection System presented in this book is based on the premise that people are the most important asset in any company. It follows, then, that the selection of people is one of the most important aspects of a manager's job. Without winners, nothing happens.

In this book, we are principally concerned with the selection and hiring of employees generally referred to as executives, managers, supervisors, and key professionals. However, the tools and techniques of the PIE system can also be applied to other levels of hiring within a company. Those aspiring to the above positions should find the information presented valuable management training to further their career.

The Seven Deadly Sins

Many of us have discovered, to our regret, that there are many pitfalls on the road to hiring a winner. We will detail the Seven Deadly Sins in the hiring of professionals, and we will show you how to avoid them. Simply put, they are:

1. *Not properly defining what is needed.* In order to find a winner, you need to be able to recognize one. The PIE System will give you the blueprints you need to do just that.
2. *Unintentionally limiting the sources for candidates.* The more sources you have to draw from, the better your chances of finding the best available person. You'll learn from this book how to increase your sourcing capabilities.
3. *Failing to interview candidates thoroughly.* Because of numerous books on the market that tell candidates how to get the jobs they want, most applicants are extremely savvy about interview techniques. The PIE System puts you back in charge.
4. *Falling for the "halo effect."* This assumes that people who are outstanding in one area will be equally outstanding in another area. The PIE System gives you the tools to assess an applicant's capabilities accurately.
5. *Wishful thinking.* This sin comes about when we desperately need a position filled. The logical steps of the PIE System do not allow this to happen.
6. *Ignoring intuition.* The PIE System encourages you to use your intuition but doesn't allow it to go unchecked.
7. *Failing to check one more reference.* After reading this book, you'll know how many references to check and how to get the information you really need when doing so.

The PIE

The PIE Selection System details a method anyone can use to find, select, and hire winners. Properly applied, it is virtually foolproof, *a total selection system* with checks and balances to ensure that nothing falls between the cracks and that you do not commit any of the Seven Deadly Sins. PIE is designed for both experienced managers and novices, and it can be put to immediate use.

PIE stands for three vital steps in the selection program:

1. *P*rofile
2. *I*nterview
3. *E*valuate

A *Profile* of your requirement specifically identifies the criteria needed to hire winners.

The in-depth *Interview* must follow a specific format to determine if the candidate matches the needs in the Profile and is thus a potential winner.

And you *Evaluate* candidates against the Profile and each other to select the best among them. They are also evaluated to ensure that what you see is what you are really going to get.

Using the PIE System, you know *what* you are looking for, *how* to find it, and how to know *when* you have found it.

In today's competitive business environment, it is vital to utilize a workable hiring system. Yet, in spite of the obvious benefits to be gained by hiring winners, most managers have had very little training, if any, in methodology designed to increase their ability to do so. Most of the available books dealing with employment discuss interviews and résumés—thus presenting only part of the full process. And many of these books look at the hiring process from the perspective of the job candidate.

To my knowledge, no college course or book on the market today teaches a total selection system that encompasses all the necessary steps needed to hire winners.

This gap in our knowledge is ironic in view of the fact that as managers we count on others to help us do our jobs. The quality of our employees reflects directly upon our own abilities. Whatever the job, our success or failure relates to the quality of people we hire.

Both you and your company can only prosper when you find good people. When you hire winners, you'll be viewed as a winner—someone with the skills and judgment needed to build a strong team—which in turn should lead to promotional opportunities and increased earnings for you.

The PIE Selection System can't guarantee that from now on you will hire only winners. But if you apply it correctly, the system will significantly minimize the sometimes expensive risks involved in hiring. PIE provides a practical, logical, step-by-step system to make your company's hiring far more predictable and far more effective.

The current competitive climate and today's emphasis on "lean, mean business machines" make it even more critical to hire winners. Hiring mistakes can damage and even disable companies, particularly when they occur at higher management levels.

Time Is Costly; So Is the Alternative

Despite all the talk about "excellence" in business management, there is little discussion about excellence in selection and hiring. And while many managers and company heads pay lip service to the concept that "people are our most valued asset," too few are willing to put their time, attention, and money where their mouths are.

In many instances, this is a costly error.

A 1985 study by the Saratoga Institute claims that the average hiring mistake costs a company $15,000. When a relocation is involved, the average cost goes up to well over $50,000.* But this is only the tip of the iceberg.

When it comes to filling management positions, experience shows that for a typical $50,000 position at least 150 hours of executive time are involved in the hiring process. Surprised to see such a high total? Well, consider the following activities that take place in a thorough selection process:

- Defining the requirements and the specific criteria to help determine exactly who and what you need
- Sourcing for candidates through advertising, recruiting firms, employee referral programs, college placement offices, or the many other approaches discussed in Chapters 5 and 6
- Reviewing applications and résumés in order to select candidates for the initial telephone interviews

*ASPA/Saratoga Institute, *Human Resource Effectiveness Survey: 1987 Annual Report* (Saratoga, Calif.: Saratoga Institute, Inc.).

- Conducting telephone interviews to determine which candidates to invite for personal interviews
- Having candidates interviewed by several executives of the company
- Interviewing the finalist candidates again, perhaps a number of times
- Meeting with the interviewers to arrive at a conclusion
- Checking the references of the three top candidates
- Negotiating an offer with the best candidate

In addition to this major investment of time, the direct costs, such as travel, relocation moves, recruiting fees, or advertising expenses are also significant. Add to this not only the post-hire time required to orient, train, and educate a new employee, but also the production time lost before the new hire functions at full efficiency. Finally, if you take into account the 20 to 30 percent that is added to the base salary for benefits costs, you can easily have a total expense that is many times the salary.

Consider further what happens if you have made a poor hiring decision: The results can range from catastrophe to aggravation—lost business opportunities, misappropriation of funds, antagonized customers, lowered company morale, even lawsuits for wrongful dismissal or negligent hiring. The latter can mean financial ruin for a company. When a company is sued because of the criminal actions of an employee, the focus of the lawyers is usually on the personnel department and the company's hiring practices. Why didn't the company screen this employee well enough to predict his criminal behavior? Unfair? Perhaps. But it is happening more often.

Many companies traditionally put more effort into the hiring of executives than of other professionals and key personnel. Companies are now becoming aware that it is also of growing importance to increase selectivity when hiring middle-level managers and professional and technical people. Today, in many parts of the country where there is a shrinking pool of talented people, it is necessary to use more sophisticated hiring practices. Those who don't take the trouble to do so simply don't get the best available workers.

Every organization wants to hire the best person for the job. That's a given. The start-up company wants a product design team to give it a technical edge, just as an independent retailer needs a store manager who meets the customer well and can perform even when the owner is absent. To each, hiring the best person for the job is crucial for success. Big corporations face exactly the same problems, although sometimes their mere size can disguise mistakes for some time.

Experience shows that of every three managers hired, one makes a solid contribution, one is marginal, and one should not have been hired in the first place. This is a fairly lamentable ratio, particularly as it flies in the face of the best of intentions. Why then does it happen?

The problem is that even though most executives have not received training in hiring decisions as part of their academic or life curriculum, they are generally expected to select and hire successful employees. This is, to say the least, unfair. Without the proper guidelines and experience, without the benefit of a workable system, how can managers be expected to define their recruitment needs, to interview candidates and determine qualifications, and to judge the potential "chemistry" the candidate would have with their team? Without helpful "tools," they are expected to make objective comparisons of a candidate's qualifications with their requirements, and then evaluate the comparisons between candidates. It's a lot to ask.

When a company reaches about one hundred employees, a human resources professional is generally brought on board. But that doesn't end potential hiring problems, even though centralized sourcing, recruiting, and preliminary screening of applicants should provide candidates to the hiring managers.

Managers still make the decisions. They cannot leave the interviewing and evaluating of candidates to anyone else. They must be able to take an involved and active role in the selection of people who will report directly to them. And herein lies a source of major failures. Most managers are just not equipped to handle these activities and or make these decisions.

Hiring and Firing

When an East Coast company was seeking a Western regional sales manager, its president, Bill S., suggested Pete, whom he had known for more than a decade and with whom he had a strong personal relationship. Pete had been in manufacturing and operations positions for over twenty years. But interviews by other company personnel quickly revealed that Pete had had no previous sales experience, nor had he stayed with one company for more than two years. Consequently, they recommended against the hire.

Bill was well aware of these shortcomings, but he felt that Pete's strong desire to sell and his sound technical knowledge of the industry from a customer's point of view—plus his obvious personal loyalty to Bill—would offset the drawbacks. In spite of the concerns, he hired Pete.

The new regional sales manager tried hard. He worked diligently to establish the company's presence in the relatively virgin Western territory. He represented the company on technical issues, solved some customers' production problems, and obtained several orders for samples. But after one year, he still had not been able to bring in one substantial new customer. It turned out that the regional sales manager could not "ask for the order" or close a sale.

Bill had to terminate his friend for lack of performance. It was no surprise to many in the company. Pete's career did not demonstrate any selling track record. A desire to sell does not necessarily make it happen.

"I Just Want a Good . . ."

Artistic Productions needed a vice-president of sales to market a new production concept that had been well received by the major film studios. Artistic faced an opportunity to increase its revenue dramatically in a short period of time.

The president, Franklyn, was a deal maker, in many ways larger than life. He talked in big numbers and frequently dropped the names of celebrities. Like many entrepreneurs, he was a concept man. And like many entrepreneurs, he tended to leave the details to his team.

Franklyn was tough to pin down. In fact, it was difficult to get him to sit still long enough to discuss his needs. "I just want a good vice-president of sales." In fact, Franklyn would have accepted any candidate who had charisma, who was aggressive, and who had a good sales track record. Then, if this new person proved to be unsuccessful at selling the new product, Franklyn would have fired him or her and hired another charismatic, aggressive salesperson. He probably would have gone through several vice-presidents before finding the right person—through sheer luck.

The world is full of Franklyns. Many executives have been hired and fired because their boss just wanted "a good manufacturing manager" or "a strong engineering director." In spite of fine records of performance prior to being hired, these managers were not able to meet the expectations of their bosses. And for good reason. The bosses did not set goals for the job and thus never specifically told the new employees what was expected of them.

Without defining the exact type of person you need to fill a position, it is almost impossible to know when you have found the right person. And without fully defining the results you expect the person to achieve—your specific needs and expectations—it is impossible to know what type of person you need. *One must first define the expectations of the position, then the experience and characteristics of the person needed to fulfill these expectations.*

With most other major expenditures—for example, the purchase of a major piece of capital equipment—a business wouldn't dream of proceeding without first defining the task that needed to be done. In the case of machinery, a clear definition of the needs or expectations allows managers to focus their inspection on equipment that could solve their problem, instead of wasting time looking at machinery that won't do the job.

Not knowing specifically what results you expect a candidate to accomplish, and thus not knowing what experience a candidate must have in order to attain these results, are the major causes of poor hiring decisions. Without this information, the selection process breaks down before it even begins.

If you want to hire a good, . . . you need to know exactly what a good . . . is.

"I Don't Have the Time"

One company recently purchased a major piece of production equipment for well over $1 million. But before making the purchase, its managers not only visited other companies that used similar equipment but also traveled to Switzerland to meet the manufacturer. They also ran a series of "what if" financial and production projections on several different pieces of potential equipment to determine exact performance expectations.

After six months of investigation and analysis, they developed specifications of what the equipment had to produce to meet their needs. Only when they knew exactly what they wanted did they place their order with the Swiss manufacturer.

Without the preliminary work and the time it involved, they might have selected the wrong equipment. Instead of gaining a competitive edge, they could have gained an expensive white elephant.

Why not be as thorough when it comes to hiring decisions? Because you don't have the time?

I've already stated that the cost of hiring a $50,000-per-year manager could amount to well in excess of $100,000. Imagine the continuing cost if rushed hiring practices and sloppy selection methods were the norm. Hiring three managers for the same job in less than a decade could cost well over $300,000!

When he hired his friend Pete as regional sales manager, Bill S. saved a lot of time by not recruiting and interviewing a vast selection of candidates. The result? Twelve months of sales effort in a virgin territory lost and months spent looking for a replacement. Lost time meant lost opportunities. The company was far behind its West Coast expansion targets. We can only guess what could have happened if Bill had taken the time to do it properly in the first place.

Selecting winners takes time. Succumbing to the pressures of short-term needs has long-term bad effects.

Of course, many managers are quite comfortable with the decision-making process involved in acquiring equipment. It is usually based on numbers and dollars—a straightforward matter of judgment, based on experience and training. However, when it comes to decisions about people, numbers are not enough, and perhaps it is not only lack of effective training but also the subjectivity involved that scare some away from doing a thorough job. Without a logical, systematic process to follow, it's easy to get lost in a maze of conflicting emotions.

The truth is that there is nothing magical about hiring winners. It doesn't take a knack or a sixth sense or even luck, just a workable system anyone can learn. With training and some experience, hiring winners can also become a straightforward matter of judgment.

A Learnable Skill

It takes very little skill and very little time to hire marginal employees, people who are not winners. The good news is that it is also easy to minimize your risks and hire winners, although it does take time and skill. Once you have learned the skills and are willing to invest the necessary time, you will no longer run the risk of hiring mediocre employees.

As pointed out earlier, interviewing is only part of the complete employee selection process. Pre- and postinterviewing activity make *all* the difference between a marginal hire and a winner.

Because it is a complete, closed-loop system, PIE allows nothing to fall between the cracks. All the tools in the PIE System tie together interdependently, and if all the steps are followed, the result will be improved hiring results.

The Profile you will learn to develop in step 1 will guide you during step 2, the Interview. At the end of step 2, depending upon what you have discovered, you will complete the Interview Evaluation Form developed from the Profile. This, coupled with the Profile, will be utilized with other tools in step 3, Evaluation.

If you skip a step, you increase your risk of hiring someone less than a winner. Each step must be followed to ensure you are tracking a winner.

A number of actions are required within each step. Each action calls for a specific result, with the final one being a winning hire.

The PIE System is not complicated. As with any skill, it needs to be practiced in order to gain fluency. Once you have gone through the process of developing a Profile, you will have no trouble repeating the process for another position. You will learn to interview with self-confidence and to evaluate the results like an expert.

The bottom line is that by using the PIE Selection System you will know how to define, find, and hire the winners you and your company need.

2

The Logic of PIE

It is commonly agreed that a manager is doing well if he or she makes correct decisions more than 50 percent of the time. Managers of top-performing companies generally exceed this percentage, which is probably what sets them and their companies apart.

Unfortunately, when it comes to employee selection, most companies do not even approach that 50-percent level of success. The selection of employees is usually an imperfect process. It often is muddled by emotions, intuition, guesses, speculation, and biases. It is predicated on people's opinions, often without hard facts to substantiate them. Small wonder, then, that it is usually a hit-and-miss proposition.

When logic is applied to this process, however, hiring suddenly becomes easier—and brings predictable results. By following a logical employee selection process, you can achieve a dramatic improvement in selecting winners and bettering your company's performance.

This logic is not all that different from the approach most rational people take when making any major purchase. Recently, I decided to buy a new camera. I didn't rush out and get the first camera a salesperson pushed at me. It was a significant purchase, one that deserved care, so I went about it very systematically.

First, I gathered data from several friends about their cameras to find out what they liked and disliked, and then I visited a number of camera stores. Although the salespeople varied in knowledge and expertise, I learned enough to decide what I would like in a camera. Finally, I came up with a list of *expectations* based upon the *results* I wanted:

1. Clear close-up *and* distant pictures
2. Pictures that would stop action
3. Fault-proof operation with minimal adjustments

Now, knowing the results I wanted, I listed four features the camera needed to get those results:

1. Automatic ASA setting when loading film
2. Automatic advancement of film
3. Automatic focus
4. Zoom lens for close-up and distance shooting

Armed with this information, I then returned to the camera stores.

Other factors entered into my decision, of course. I also considered the opinions of friends and camera store salespeople, the design and feel of the camera, price, and warranty. But when I determined exactly what I wanted the camera to do, the decision was easier.

We all go through some degree of decision making when purchasing something, particularly when it requires a significant outlay of money. It is just a logical, commonsense, necessary approach.

The PIE Selection System was designed to provide just such a logical framework for employee selection.

The PIE Ingredients

The first step in the PIE System is the *Profile,* which is essentially an in-depth analysis of the *specific results* you wish to achieve by filling the vacant position, and then of the kind of person who could achieve those results. In a sense, then, the PIE System begins at the end, with the result. This is the often-overlooked foundation of the entire hiring process.

People are often hired for positions because of certain qualifications listed on their résumé. Even when these qualifications match the job description, this is not good enough. It's like buying a camera with the only requirement being that it take 35mm pictures. The exact *needs,* the results you want, are not considered.

The first step in developing your Profile is to create a list of *performance expectations*—specific results you expect someone in the position to achieve. For instance, you may need a research chemist to develop two new products during the next twelve months. This is a measurable result.

In another instance, you may need an employment manager to develop a significant recruitment program that will double your production work force from four hundred to eight hundred employees during the next two years. This is also a measurable result. It can be quantified further into quarterly and annual objectives.

Using your list of performance expectations, you then develop *success patterns* and *personal characteristics*—accomplishments and traits (much like the camera features) that a candidate should have in order to meet the expectations. A success pattern might be "Experienced in developing and implementing a major recruitment program for production employees, which resulted in the successful hiring of at least two hundred employees within one year." A personal characteristic could be "Excellent written and oral communication skills." Again, these are specific, measurable, and verifiable accomplishments and traits.

Together, these three elements make up the Profile (requirements of person to be hired and the job defined in terms of attainable results), as diagrammed in Figure 1.

The PIE System does not begin with or even use job descriptions. The duties and responsibilities that usually make up job descriptions are often vague and not really measurable. The PIE System is concerned with your specific needs and the specific results you want the candidate to achieve.

Experience shows that every job can be defined in terms of results, whether it involves a plant manager in a chemical company, a president of a financial institution, a cost accounting

Figure 1. Key elements of the Profile.

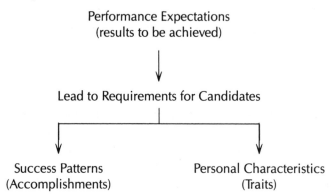

manager with an appliance manufacturer, or a research engineer in an electronics company.

Some people ask how one can set up performance expectations for a research position. "You can't tell them that you want a particular result by a certain time," one president claimed. Well, you can. In fact, you must tell them what is expected; otherwise it will be difficult to judge whether or not they are good at what they do.

When a vice-president of research and development was hired by a producer of materials for the electronics industry, the company did not simply look for a person to head the department in charge of developing products. That would not have defined the desired results. Instead, the company said that there were certain products that needed to be developed in a certain time frame and within a certain budget.

In this manner, the company was able to hire a person who had many of the success patterns and personal characteristics needed to meet this challenge. The performance expectations were reviewed with the candidates with the purpose of gaining agreement that the results could be achieved. Because of the precise Profile developed, the chosen candidate did indeed turn out to be a winner.

The Profile is similar in many ways to the concept of management by objectives (MBO), a management style that includes the mutual development of, and agreement on, specific objectives against which to measure a person's performance. This common management practice is not often used in the recruiting process, but it should be. In fact, it is the underlying basis of the PIE System.

Everything you do in developing the Profile is essential to the next two major steps, *Interview* and *Evaluate*.

What you look for in your candidates is based upon what you have defined in the Profile. This gives each interview a defined goal: to find out how closely the candidate matches the Profile. Interviewers who simply follow the résumé, thus learning nothing new about the candidate, do not really discover whether or not the candidate is suited for the position.

While the interview process is comfortable for some people, for many it is an intimidating experience. In this book, you will find an interviewing style and procedure that is effective and easy for anyone to learn. This style will facilitate your discovery of the success patterns and personal characteristics.

The president of a small but growing manufacturing company used to complete his interview of a potential executive in about twenty minutes. Following a technique of asking pointed, challenging questions, he quickly formed strong opinions about each candidate. But he had absolutely no idea how the person arrived at the answers or the actual thought process involved. The interview consisted of direct answers to direct questions. At the end of an interview this president knew very little about the candidate. By the same token, the people being interviewed did not know much about the company or their potential boss. What they did know was that the man apparently wasn't interested enough to find out their real abilities and accomplishments. No rapport, no real communication, had been established.

The president was actually intimidated by the interviewing experience. His solution to his discomfort was to adopt an aggressive attitude and fire a series of pointed questions in order to get the interview over with as quickly as possible. Things improved after he attained and practiced better interviewing skills. As he grew more comfortable and effective, interviews became a way for him to acquire and exchange meaningful information. And they typically lasted 90 to 120 minutes. It was a dramatic change—one that made a major difference in the quality of personnel he hired.

In Chapters 9, 10, and 11, we discuss interviewing in greater detail. Some of the areas examined include:

- Should interviewing be done by one person or several?
- How can you get the information you want?
- How do you determine a person's success patterns and personal characteristics, and what do they mean?
- How do you compare what you find to the Profile?
- How can you improve your ability to judge candidates?
- What are some probing questions and techniques to use?
- What questions must you avoid?

At the conclusion of each interview, you will complete a Candidate Evaluation Form (see Figure 3, Chapter 14). This form is specifically designed so that you can objectively record your immediate impressions and conclusions regarding the candidate's success patterns and personal characteristics. After following this form step by step, you will have a clear understanding of whether the candidate is someone you should pursue.

During the final step of the PIE System, the Evaluation section, you will use the Candidate Evaluation Form to compare each candidate to the Profile and to the other candidates. Then you will utilize your newly acquired interview skills to check references and verify all the information you have gained thus far, once again referring all results back to the Profile.

Anyone Can Do It

The PIE Selection System works for small, large, and in-between companies.

In a small company, the manager or owner typically develops the Profile; in a large company, it may be someone from the human resources department *in conjunction* with the relevant supervisor.

The team approach may be utilized in interviewing candidates. For some positions, in addition to the supervisor, as many as two, three, or more management people might also interview the leading candidates. In those cases, the interviewers can compare notes in order to reach a consensus.

If there are people in your company who aspire to management positions, part of their supervisory training should be how to select and hire people. Indeed, exercises in developing Profiles encourage your employees to think about their jobs in terms of accomplishments rather than activities. Remember that winners are results/accomplishments driven.

What Results to Expect

"What percentage of the people you have hired should not have been hired in the first place?"

Answers to informal surveys of that question range from 25 to 50 percent. On average, managers say that about one-third of the people they have hired should not have been hired at all.

Assuming this is accurate, what about the other two-thirds? Typical survey responses indicate that about half of them are winners—major contributors—and about half are marginal employees who just about meet minimum expectations.

It would be nice if you could always hire winners. The reality is that no company has a 100-percent winning work force: There just aren't enough winners to go around. By improving your selection skills, however, you will hire fewer people who "should not have been hired in the first place."

What difference could this make in your business? What are the potential results of a logical, systematic approach to hiring?

Let's start with the premise that your company's selection of employees is about average: One-third of them are winners, one-third are marginal, and one-third should not have been hired.

For demonstration purposes, let's also assume that winners contribute at the rate of 10, marginal employees at the rate of 5, and others at the rate of 2. (We'll assume that you don't hire employees who "contribute" at a negative rate.)

Let's further assume that there are 99 employees. What would their total contribution be?

	Employees	Contribution Level	Employee Contribution
Winners	33	10	330
Marginals	33	5	165
Others	33	2	66
Total employee contribution			561

Now your company needs to expand and must hire 33 additional employees. If you continued your present hiring practices, you would still hire one-third of each type of employee, and the total contribution would be as follows:

	Employees	Contribution Level	Employee Contribution
Winners	44	10	440
Marginals	44	5	220
Others	44	2	88
Total employee contribution			748

Employment increased by 33 percent, as did total employee contribution. But what if you had hired only winners and marginals, equally divided between the two categories? In that case, the total contribution would have been entirely different.

	Employees	Contribution Level	Employee Contribution
Winners	49	10	490
Marginals	50	5	250
Others	33	2	66
Total employee contribution			806

Employment still rose 33 percent, but total contribution rose by almost 44 percent! Average contribution per employee increased by 7 percent.

You may question the relative validity of the assigned contribution levels. Admittedly, they are only rough estimates. Nevertheless, it becomes very clear that when you increase the number of winners and marginals you hire, overall contribution improves dramatically. If you were able to hire only winners, the results would be even more impressive.

Studying and implementing an employee selection process using the PIE System will certainly increase the capabilities of the employees you hire and, consequently, the contributions of your company's work force.

3

The Profile Is Basic

It's difficult, if not impossible, to hire effective people without using the Profile. As the foundation of the PIE System, the Profile defines your requirements. It delineates not only the functions in the company that need to be addressed but also the results needed to make that company successful. By examining these results, it enables us to look at the requirements in terms of a person who can fulfill them.

The Profile enables you to know ahead of time what kind of person will be best suited for the position you're trying to fill. Without it, you're left with only the hope that you'll know a winner when he or she walks through the door. It is the key to the whole selection process, yet it is often the most neglected step.

In defining the requirements for a particular job, the Profile also forces a company to look at its needs in a realistic light and, if necessary, to reevaluate them.

Take the example of a well-known show business trade publication that wanted to increase advertising revenue. When one of the board members suggested that this could be accomplished by hiring a vice-president of sales, the magazine's owners indicated their willingness to create a new executive position with a compensation of more than $70,000 a year.

As the publication's executives attempted to develop a Profile for this vice-president, however, the real need appeared. Their emphasis was totally on sales, not on typical management responsibilities. There was no mention of the objectives to recruit, motivate, or direct a sales group. Thus, what they needed was three more commission salespeople to produce revenue. The owners could continue to act as the vice-president of sales.

Situations like this are not uncommon. A company's managers will say they want a chief financial officer when their real need is for a strong general accounting manager. This is not to say that the accounting manager could not become the CFO. The point is that the results to be achieved should be used to determine what kind of person will be sought. The results you would expect from a CFO are generally broader than what you would expect of an accounting manager.

One reason for mistakes like these is that companies take their main hiring guidelines from job descriptions or titles, which describe or imply a candidate's duties and responsibilities instead of defining results.

The employment section of any newspaper carries scores of advertisements that describe duties and responsibilities, typically taken from a job description. Only the rare ad will specify what results the employer desires to achieve by hiring someone for that position.

The fact is that job descriptions don't do the job. They don't tell the employer what to look for in a candidate, and they don't tell the candidate what the job is really about. Job descriptions are usually based upon past performance and thus do not necessarily reflect the needs of the present or the future. Job descriptions in effect encourage a company to remain historical, tied to the past. Companies need flexibility to get things accomplished, in today's competitive climate.

Performance Expectations— Getting What You Need

The first step in developing a workable Profile is to list your performance expectations. What will filling this position actually accomplish for the company? What are the needs to be fulfilled? What will be the desired results?

Results are synonymous with accomplishments, whereas job descriptions merely reflect activities, which may be "blue smoke and mirrors" designed to disguise or hide an employee's confusion and ineptitude. It's easy enough to appear busy, making phone calls, attending meetings, writing reports, and questioning staff. These activities may or may not lead to accomplishments.

However, listing goals—"Today I'm going to get a $50,000 order and develop one new customer" or "I'm going to find a method to reduce the cost of manufacturing this widget by 5 percent"—means talking about results and accomplishments, not mere activity.

Some people who seem to do very little actually accomplished significant results by the end of the day. Others, who constantly generate a smokescreen of activity, moving papers from in basket to out basket, accomplish nothing. Even though they have created a lot of action, they have achieved little in the way of results.

When you measure performance in terms of results, it's very hard to hide a gaping hole of ineptitude in a company.

A job description for a company controller might read that the duties include "responsibility for managing the cost accounting function, accounts payable, accounts receivable, and general ledger, being able to close the books in a timely manner, and reporting to management." This, of course, doesn't tell you specifically how to measure the effectiveness of whoever holds that job. Usually the fact that the person has experience in these areas is impetus enough to hire him or her.

As an example, what exactly does it mean to say that a person is responsible for the cost accounting function? In developing the performance expectations for this controller, you could state one result you expect from the cost accounting function as "to determine the actual manufacturing costs of products A and B." When talking about closing the books, you might indicate that you want "the books to be closed by the tenth of each month."

Now you have something measurable, specific expectations that you can discuss with the candidates. You are now in a position to say to them, "If you can consistently close the books by the tenth of the month, you'll be a hero. If you do it by the twelfth of the month, you haven't made the grade.''

Descriptions of sales positions also tend to focus on duties and responsibilities. A typical job description of a regional sales manager might include "responsible for sales in his territory; for managing and motivating the sales force; for developing good customer relations; for increasing sales; and for bringing in new accounts.'' These are all rather vaguely worded descriptions; there are no sharply defined results.

A more effective approach to this job might be to say that results should include "a sales increase of 22 percent in the coming year, while maintaining the same profit margin.'' As for managing the sales force, a performance expectation might be "to reduce cost of sales from 6.5 percent of annual sales to 6 percent of annual sales.'' That is a measurable goal, as is "evaluate each sales representative organization to ensure they are all producing at least $100,000 in sales every quarter.'' Descriptions of duties and responsibilities are not really measurable, thus do not give you the benefit of being able to judge performance.

All jobs are quantifiable. You can even take a position as seemingly unmeasurable as research engineer and evaluate performance. One approach to this would be to establish as a goal for the research engineer the development of three potential new products within the next twelve months. Now you have something measurable against which to evaluate performance. If the engineer works all year and doesn't produce any new products, you could reasonably question why you hired him or her. Of course, you would not typically wait until the end of the year for the products to appear. Instead, you would review progress and expectations at least quarterly, making appropriate adjustments or taking other action.

The easiest way to develop your expectations is to examine the results you want to achieve. One method is to pose a hypothetical situation for yourself: If you had hired that person last year, what results would you have expected him or her to have achieved by today?

Developing a Profile is also a good tool to use if and when you need to hire a consultant. Consider the example of one firm that was looking to hire a public relations consultant. This company had never used the services of any public relations firm but knew what results it wanted to achieve. The question was, Were their expectations realistic?

The company interviewed several public relations firms and freelance consultants, inviting each to review the performance expectations. The president asked all the consultants to comment on the viability of the results he expected and to say how they would go about achieving those results. Their answers and approach to meeting his requirements gave him sufficient insight to help him make a hiring decision.

People are usually hired for one of two reasons: to replace someone who has left or to fill a new position created because the company is expanding or needs to acquire technology or capability. In developing your performance expectations, you are forced to ask yourself if you really need anyone at all. You may find that the talent already exists in the company, in the person of a current employee or even several people. You may not need to hire anyone new.

There are also times when you find that your expectations are unrealistic. The company's desire to expand might not match its current capabilities. In other instances, the expectations might be too low.

Take the example of a start-up software company whose president, Phil, was the creative, well-educated inventor of a proprietary software product. He was an optimist in terms of business, an idealist in terms of personnel. He came from an academic environment and had never been in an entrepreneurial situation.

Phil developed a Profile for the position of vice-president of sales that listed performance expectations in terms of revenues at x level. Contrary to the advice of some of his board, Phil hired a sales vice-president who was not familiar with the company's targeted market. No one was really sure why Phil had hired him. Perhaps some of the "idealist" was coming through.

The candidate had agreed with Phil on the revenue projections in the Profile. Unfortunately, both Phil and the candidate were off—by tenfold. Perhaps the company didn't understand the market; or the product wasn't ready to meet the customer's needs; or the new sales vice-president wasn't able to make it happen. Certainly, the expectations proved to be very unrealistic.

Whatever the result, the exercise of developing performance expectations for particular positions in your company will give you a better understanding of both your needs and your goals. It forces you to examine your true situation in a clear, realistic light.

Noncongruent Expectations

When the expectations of the employee do not match the expectations of the employer, we call them noncongruent expectations. This lapse of communication occurs often when Profiles are not developed for positions.

A small manufacturing company hired a sales representative firm for the Southwest territory. One performance expectation was that the rep firm produce sales at a rate of $300,000 a year, but the manufacturing company failed to communicate this to the reps. Instead of being specific, the company sales manager had said, "We need you to provide a strong sales effort for us this year. You need to make sure that all the accounts in your territory are covered. Let's really see some results! We want sales!"

By the end of the year, the new reps had done just what was asked of them—they had developed a strong sales presence in the territory and had visited all the accounts—but they had only produced sales of $50,000. The rep firm believed it had done a good job, but the president of the manufacturing company was very disappointed. His expectations and the rep firm's expectations had been noncongruent.

This scenario frequently happens when expectations are not clearly understood by both parties. It sets up both parties to lose/lose instead of win/win.

On the individual level, too, excellent executives are often fired because they haven't lived up to expectations. But in cases of noncongruent expectations, the executives probably thought they were doing well even as the company managers found their performance lacking. When expectations are not communicated in terms of measurable results, both parties lose.

A machinery company in the Midwest hired a vice-president of sales. The president was very clear about what he wanted—an increase in sales and a reduction in costs. One year later, the vice-president of sales got an excellent bonus based on her achieving the performance expectations. However, when one of the directors asked the president what new customers the vice-president had brought in during that twelve-month period, he said, "None. She increased sales with existing customers." The director then asked the president if he didn't want new customers to expand his base. He replied, "Of course I do."

"Why didn't she bring in new customers?" probed the director.

The president thought a moment and then said, "Well, I guess I really didn't spell that out as a specific expectation."

The president subsequently met with his vice-president and told her of the need to get new accounts and capture new markets in addition to increasing existing markets.

The president was obviously at fault for not defining everything he wanted. Noncongruent expectations are generally either not identified or, if identified, are not made known to the person responsible for fulfilling them.

With the PIE System you usually give the leading candidates a copy of the performance expectations before the hiring decision, enabling them to know what results are expected. (You will see later that it is also a good problem-solving task during the interview to ask all candidates how they would go about accomplishing those results.) If you don't communicate your expectations, you can't expect them to be accomplished.

4

Blueprint for a Winner

Once defined, performance expectations—the results we expect to have accomplished—lead to the next step of the Profile. Because we understand the expectations, we now have the information needed to develop a list of what we want in a person.

What must this person have in order to accomplish these performance expectations?

The answer falls into two categories: success patterns and personal characteristics.

Success Patterns

The PIE System is based upon the simple premise that people will generally do in the future what they have done in the past. They have a track record that can be judged.

In essence, a person's success patterns are made up of (1) experiences, (2) accomplishments, and (3) skills. All of these patterns indicate whether or not an individual will be able to meet the performance expectations or results we have identified.

Let's translate this concept into practical terms. Every company sells something, tangible or intangible, so let's use an example of a salesperson for a computer systems company. What might be some of the performance expectations for this position?

We could expect this person:

- To produce sales of $50,000–$75,000 a month in the first year
- To sell to colleges, which form our customer base
- To increase sales by 20–30 percent a year in the region—the Western United States

In order to find someone to fulfill this list of performance expectations, what success patterns should we look for and define? For the purposes of this example, let's assume that the computer systems are selling for about $25,000 each. In order to meet the expectation of $75,000 a month, three systems must be sold.

Therefore:

1. The first success pattern to look for would be: *experience selling computer systems.*
2. We don't want someone who is used to selling computer systems in the $1,000–$2,000 range—that doesn't indicate an ability to sell a $25,000 item—so we would look for: *experience selling products or systems in the $25,000 and higher price range.*
3. We want someone with experience selling to our customer base, so the third pattern we would look for is: *experience selling to the college market.*
4. Perhaps a further success pattern would be evidence that the person has increased sales by as much as 20–30 percent a year. Therefore, we would look for: *a track record of increasing sales by at least 20 percent annually.*
5. And still a fifth success pattern might be: *familiarity with the Western United States sales region.*

The idea is to match these success patterns with the candidate's experience. It's like putting one grid on top of another. You are looking for comparable patterns. People who have all or most of these success patterns in their background have a good chance of being successful in this job.

One has to use a considerable amount of judgment when it comes to the final analysis of how well a candidate matches the success patterns. It is not always possible or necessary for the grids to match exactly. Each position has its own needs.

In the example above, for instance, it may not be vitally important for all the candidates to have sold *computer systems* to colleges. It may be just as important that they have called on colleges and know the market for your products. In fact, some candidates may never have sold a computer system. A proven sales record for something like high-priced audiovisual systems in the same market just might do.

Of course, in comparing one candidate to another, all other things being equal, the person with the most success patterns should be a step ahead.

Ten Times One, or Does One Equal Ten?

"I need a topnotch manager with at least ten years of experience." You've heard that one before. The assumption is that years of experience alone make the difference. But what is really important about those ten years of experience? You need to find out if it was a decade of repeating the same job every year or of continual learning and growing.

Success patterns are never defined by a specific number of years of experience. What matters is what the candidate has accomplished or achieved relative to the experience required. Perhaps one candidate achieved the result in three years and another candidate did it in five years. The important aspect is that the result was achieved. Then the question arises, "Why did it take one person two more years to get to the same place?" That would be the area to pursue. Two more years of experience may not have added anything to that person's career except time.

People's careers progress at varying speeds. Capability and opportunity may be the governing factors that determine the span of experience. A person with one year of experience may be just as capable as a person with one year of experience repeated ten times.

You must trace success patterns throughout the person's life. Note examples of accomplishments, experiences, and skills that may coincide with the success patterns you have established based on the results we need, the performance expectations.

Keep in mind that as you work with a newly hired employee, you may modify your expectations. In fact, as mentioned earlier, it is wise to at least review them quarterly. Nothing is cast in concrete. By looking at jobs in terms of expectations, you develop a certain amount of flexibility to meet goals.

The number of success patterns for a position will depend on the number of performance expectations. You should have at least one success pattern for each of the performance expectations, and you might have more than one success pattern for a specific expectation.

You now know what you need the person to accomplish (performance expectations) and what your candidates must have accomplished in the past (success patterns) to make this a realistic goal. But what type of person is best do the job? What personality characteristics, traits, or work habits should the individual have in order to meet the performance expectations? This brings us to the personal characteristics of each individual.

Personal Characteristics

A mergers and acquisitions consulting firm in the Midwest recently hired a vice-president to put deals together. He is an exemplary employee—hard-working, innovative, and responsible. The only problem is that he doesn't like to fly and his job requires frequent travel throughout the United States.

The company has a problem. It may soon have to look for another vice-president. Unfortunately, this aversion to flying is a personal characteristic that was missed in the selection process.

As with success patterns, personal characteristics are to be discovered and probed during the interview. The personal characteristics of a successful salesperson, for instance, could call for someone who is tenacious, who is motivated by accomplishment in terms of sales, who is not easily rejected, who makes good presentations, who has excellent communication skills, and who can establish personal rapport. On the other hand, if you are looking for an accountant, you might want someone who is analytical, detail-oriented, and well organized.

As part of developing a Profile, it would be a good idea on a corporate level for all the company managers to get together and actually develop a list of personal characteristics required of every person joining the company at a certain level. For example, if your company is aggressive, a personal characteristic of most candidates should be aggressiveness. If you are a high-energy, fast-moving organization, those traits should also be candidate requirements. Integrity is another characteristic you would want in anyone you hire.

Every company should have a generic list of personal characteristics that virtually define the personality and image of the company—what it is, what image it presents to the outside world. These characteristics can be developed from past experience and observation. In time, most people will be able to make judgments as to what kind of personality fits best into their company.

Perhaps the best method is to study the current winners in your organization. Once you know the personal characteristics common to the most important, productive, and efficient members of the company, you will have a set of standards against which you can judge candidates for employment.

These characteristics might differ somewhat from position to position, but there should be a generic base that defines the type of people you want. Most of these characteristics could be a matter of chemistry, as described immediately below, but the result will be a statement about what kind of people would fit into and contribute to the current organization.

Chemistry

"She just wasn't our type of manager."
"He couldn't adapt to our way of thinking."
"He didn't fit in with our management team."
"The chemistry wasn't there."

Chemistry implies an interaction between people, a measure of compatibility of styles, and a seeking of common goals and/or objectives.

"Good chemistry" within a management group means that the team works well together toward reaching its goals. It does not indicate that all members of the team look alike, think alike, or even like one another, or that they perform their tasks in the same manner and at the same speed.

The importance of the management team as a group cannot be overemphasized. Most venture capitalists who are deciding whether or not to invest in a small company will turn quickly to the pages of a business plan that contain the résumés of the management team. They want to know the experience of the key players and if this team can work well together. Does their chemistry make them a fit?

When I look back on the scores of lists of personal characteristics developed with clients over the years, the one characteristic that almost always appears is "Must have 'chemistry' with company management team." Of course, that personal characteristic has little meaning by itself unless the interviewers know the management chemistry of the company.

Typically, the chemistry is revealed in many of the other personal characteristics that are developed. A good example of this is found in a successful West Coast manufacturing firm. At one of their retreats senior management developed a list of characteristics that should be evident in all the managers hired by the company. A look at some of these characteristics reveals the chemistry of the company.

Managerial Characteristics

1. A sense of urgency
2. Good health and an ability to handle stress
3. Enthusiasm and a positive attitude
4. Self-confidence
5. Customer-orientation and quality-mindedness
6. Ability to accept direction as well as delegate
7. Good planning and implementation skills
8. Creativity and resourcefulness

9. Commitment to corporate success
10. Commitment to doing a job right the first time
11. A no-nonsense attitude and results orientation

This list was a composite of both how the managers viewed themselves at that time *and* how they wanted to develop the management team of the future.

The company's goals and objectives led to the development of this list. Had the goals and objectives been different at that time, the list would have reflected those differences. Consequently, the chemistry of a company is dynamic, changing to meet the targeted goals. And this change in chemistry is reflected in the personal characteristics.

If you are hiring a senior management person, one of the personal characteristics you seek might be a compatible "chemistry" between this person and the rest of your management team.

In fact, start-up companies are often formed by individuals who have worked well together in the past. Part of their success will depend on the chemistry between the key players. Knowing their management style and their compatibility with one another, as well as their mutual interest in achieving goals, should help you put together a strong management team. However, a previous history of working together does not guarantee successful chemistry. For example, people who have worked well together in a large company may not always be as compatible in a start-up situation, where the problems and pressures are quite different.

What's the Formula?

The chemistry of a candidate is an important factor to consider when building or adding to a management team. How, then, do you determine whether the chemistry between a candidate and the management team is compatible?

First, you must determine the chemistry of your management team. How do they interact? What is the prevailing management style? How do you foresee it changing in the future? These are some of the questions you need to answer in order to develop a list of personal characteristics common to all managers within the company.

Second, you need to develop questions and problem-solving exercises that will bring out these characteristics (or lack of them) during interviews with the candidates. Many of these questions are mentioned in Chapters 10 and 11.

Finally, you need to verify these characteristics as part of your reference-checking procedure.

A management candidate's chemistry with the management team for which he or she is being considered can be assessed in other ways. Note how a candidate reacts outside the pressure of an interview. Going to a restaurant or a sports event *after* interviews have been completed may afford you an opportunity to witness the rest of the story.

The spouse or significant other may also shed some light on work habits, management style, and "who" *really* makes the decisions.

Whether you are recruiting an executive for a small company or a large corporation, compatible "chemistry" is a key factor that can determine whether you have a winner *for your environment*.

Absolutes and Pluses

In a typical Profile, you may have eight to twelve success patterns and a similar number of personal characteristics that you are seeking in a candidate. If you wanted to find one candidate with all of the success patterns and all of the personal characteristics, you could be looking for a lifetime. The fact is that you might never find someone with all of these attributes. You can still find a winner, however.

The PIE System solution to this dilemma is to review all of the personal characteristics and success patterns and judge them against the performance expectations. Then you have to determine the relative importance of each personal characteristic and success pattern to see which are absolutes and which are pluses.

An absolute is a success pattern or personal characteristic that candidates must have in order to be considered for the position. These attributes are absolutely necessary. (Keep in mind that you may not know for certain whether a candidate has all the absolutes until after the interview and you have had a chance to check references.)

Experience shows that about four or, at most, five success patterns and the same number of personal characteristics are sufficient to identify these "knockout" factors. Throughout the screening process—résumé review, phone and personal interviews, references—if you determine that an absolute is missing, you then should eliminate the candidate *or* determine whether your absolutes may be unrealistic and need rethinking.

Which success patterns become absolutes? This is difficult to define for a job without knowing the particulars of the position. Let's return to the example of the computer products salesperson.

The company managers might feel an absolute is that the candidate must have experience selling to their particular market, which is at colleges and universities. The person must know the buyers and other decision makers in the higher education market.

On the other hand, the requirement that the candidate be experienced in the sale of computer systems may not be an absolute. It might suffice for a candidate to have sold something else, such as big-ticket video equipment, to colleges. Therefore, the success pattern of selling computer products might not be an absolute, though it would be a plus—an important but not absolutely necessary background, quality, or achievement.

You must make these distinctions between absolutes and pluses, otherwise you could eliminate every candidate who steps up to your door.

When you compare candidates, the differences between them are often related to how many pluses they each have. As noted, it's likely that all your finalists will have all the absolutes. Thus, the candidate who has more pluses than the others may have the edge.

Absolutes and pluses are a way of deciding which personal characteristics and success patterns are most important. They will help you screen candidates over the telephone before you even interview them. And often you can even identify the lack of absolutes in a person's résumé or application. Thus you can quickly pare your list of candidates down to those who are worth pursuing.

Absolutes and pluses are only one of the available tools to use in selecting candidates. There are other ways to measure candidates against your lists of personal characteristics and success patterns. You could assign rankings or weightings to each success pattern and personal characteristic. Something that is an absolute could be worth a 5, something that is desirable a 3, and the others may all carry a 1. This method serves a purpose similar to that of the absolutes and pluses.

A word of caution: When you come up with a numerical score for each candidate, it carries certain dangers, particularly if it is a close call. (Later, in Chapter 14, we'll talk about intuition—a factor that numbers cannot really take into consideration.) A numerical score for a candidate cannot provide your ultimate answer.

I have seen situations where a candidate who meets all the absolutes is passed over for a candidate who doesn't appear to have all the requirements but who has certain more impressive strengths. Unless you feel very comfortable using a numerical system, you would do better to utilize a system of absolutes and pluses. It has proved to be more flexible and, thus, more workable.

The owners of an Eastern electronics distribution company wanted to make an offer to a highly energetic, bright, and talented human resources executive even though she did not have all the success patterns that were in the Profile. So they rethought the list of absolutes and decided that the "chemistry" between the candidate and their management team was more important than the experience requirements they had initially defined. If they had employed a strictly numerical scoring system, they might not have offered this candidate the position.

The above example also points out that a Profile is never "cast in concrete." In fact, it is not uncommon to find that a modification in the Profile—perhaps in the performance expectations and thus in the required success patterns—results after interviewing several candidates. In the human resources managerial recruitment effort cited, "chemistry" became a more

significant selection factor after the company had interviewed
several candidates.

Making the Profile Work for You

The development of a Profile is not just an academic exercise to
help you sort out your thoughts; it is a practical tool that can be
fully utilized in the real world of candidate selection.

It can be helpful in many ways. First of all, as you will see
from the example of a Profile at the end of this chapter, it is
written in a standard format. It gives you a place to write out all
the information you have gathered so that your requirements
will be logically collated, easily understandable, and readily
applicable. The Profile is then used to develop an Interview
Evaluation Form so that you can complete a summary evaluation
of the candidate after an interview.

Each individual who is going to interview and evaluate the
candidates should have a copy of the Profile. In this way each
person has written answers to the question "What am I looking
for in this candidate?" in obvious and standardized form. Keep
in mind that the Profile shows *exactly* what to look for during
the interview. The success patterns indicate what experience
and skills need to be present, while the personal characteristics
show the traits necessary to accomplish the performance expectations.

Further along in the selection process, the Profile's performance expectations should be shown to the finalist candidates. This should obviate the problem of noncongruent expectations, which we discussed earlier. If shown the performance
expectations, the candidates know your exact expectations and
how they are being measured. To make sure of this, you might
ask each candidate to comment on the expectations. Are they
"doable"? How would he or she approach the task of meeting
the expectations? What would the candidate need to know in
order to determine if these expectations could be met? Showing the candidates the performance expectations is not unlike
giving them a problem to solve. (This will be discussed later in
Chapter 11.)

Can you get into trouble showing the total Profile to a

candidate? Perhaps. The success patterns might give some candidates sufficient information to bias their presentations to you.
And rejected candidates could ask why they weren't hired even
though they had met all the criteria. (The explanation here is
usually that the other candidate had more or better credentials.)
In general, it is much more desirable to just show the candidates
only the list of performance expectations, not the entire Profile.

Putting It All Together

You will gain a clear understanding of the information in this
chapter once you have applied it to a practical situation. It's like
reading a book on how to develop a strong tennis backhand: The
theory seems logical, but until you actually grasp the racket
correctly and practice your swing and stance, you won't have a
chance to perfect the stroke. The same holds true in the development of a Profile. There is no better lesson than sitting down
and actually doing your first Profile. However, before you do
that, study the following example of what a Profile looks like.

Let's take an imaginary company called the Alpha Corporation and develop a Profile for the position of Western regional
sales manager.

Alpha Corporation

ALPHA CORPORATION is a computer systems company that sells
a turnkey package to the academic market—colleges and
universities. It purchases the hardware components and mod-
ifies them to accept its software, producing a unique system.
Founded three years ago by Stanford Professor Jack Carter,
Alpha now enjoys revenues of approximately $3 million
annually.

The company has had a regional sales manager for the
Eastern half of the United States for about one year. With the
headquarters located in Palo Alto, California, sales for the
Western half of the country have been managed by the vice-
president of sales.

The business outlook is promising, with sales forecasts for the coming year budgeted at $5 million.

Assuming an equal distribution of revenues between East and West, this would represent revenues of $2.5 million from each region. To achieve this target, it was decided to hire a Western regional sales manager who could make a full-time effort producing sales.

ALPHA CORPORATION

PROFILE: REGIONAL SALES MANAGER

PERFORMANCE EXPECTATIONS (Results we expect to accomplish within the first year by having someone in this position)

1. Will increase sales to an average of $210,000 per month over the twelve-month period
2. Will obtain orders from a minimum of ten new accounts
3. Will maintain cost of sales to less than 5 percent of gross sales for this region
4. Will provide management, on a weekly basis, with call report activity on customers and prospects, indicating sales opportunities, follow-up commitments, and new product ideas
5. Will ensure that each new customer receives systems training according to established schedules
6. Will promptly handle all customer problems in a satisfactory manner

To accomplish the above performance expectations, candidates should have the following success patterns and personal characteristics.

Success Patterns

1. Have a track record of personally generating sales of at least $2 million annually*

2. Have experience in selling computer systems to end-user organizations

3. Have experience in selling sophisticated equipment to universities and colleges*

4. Have a track record of developing new accounts*

5. Have a college degree*

6. Have experience in solving customer problems and establishing solid customer relations

Personal Characteristics

1. Have integrity and honesty*

2. Have a high energy level

3. Have good verbal communication skills and strong, positive personal presence*

4. Have drive, tenacity, and the determination to win*

5. Have a strong customer orientation

6. Have compatible "chemistry" with the management team*

7. Be well organized

8. Be a self-starter*

*Absolutes: The patterns and characteristics that are absolutely required are indicated with an asterisk (*). Without these absolutes, a person will not be considered. The other attributes, not so indicated, are pluses—highly desirable success patterns and personal characteristics that can be used to differentiate between candidates.

This, then, is the Alpha Corporation Profile for a Western regional sales manager. It defines the desirable results and exactly what is needed to accomplish these results. The company now knows what to look for in every candidate. There is no need for wishing and hoping and guessing.

We will return to Alpha and observe this Profile in action later in this book.

5

Find 'Em

Once you have developed your Profile and know your exact needs and the type of person likely to fill them, your next step is to locate a wide variety of candidates. Your search should begin as early as possible so that you will be able to find a large number of people from whom to select your winner.

There are plenty of good sources of qualified candidates. They may be divided into two basic categories—current employees and everyone else. This chapter will provide general guidelines for searching both categories, while the next chapter will provide a list of specific sources for you to explore. The more creative and resourceful you are willing to be, the more candidates you will find.

Looking Within

The natural place to look first is within your own company. This is sometimes faster and less expensive than going outside, and promotions of existing staff are usually good for company morale. However, such a course does have drawbacks. The biggest danger is that you won't go through a candidate-selection process but will simply choose the one candidate who *seems* ideal. By staying inside the company, you might not find the best available candidate for the position. However, if you develop your Profile and find an in-house person to match it, he or she should be strongly considered along with other candidates.

An extremely valuable asset for every company to have is some kind of skills bank of their current employees. It may be as basic as a file of three-by-five-inch cards or as complex as a computerized program. The skills bank should contain files of all the people within the company, with information on their backgrounds before they joined you as well as on their progress within the company. In some very small companies, a skills bank boils down to the president knowing most of the people in the organization.

When a position opens, the skills bank enables you to review your existing assets quickly and compare their qualifications to your Profile. You may well have someone who can be promoted to the position, or, as many companies do today, you may subscribe to the theory of cross-training. For example, you might move someone from manufacturing to a new position in engineering. Cross-training increases the capabilities of your existing employees and, thus, their value to the company.

Another method of using a company's existing human resources is to have understudies for key positions. People who are next in line for these positions within the organization can serve a kind of apprenticeship. When an opening occurs, they can move into the vacant spot.

Some companies make it a point to post notices of all openings for employees to review. This has a dual advantage in that an employee may apply for the position or may refer someone else. The caution needed in such a practice is that you must be prepared to explain to employee applicants why they were not accepted when that is the case.

It's a good rule of thumb to fill at least 20 percent of your jobs from outside the company. New people stimulate new ideas and competition, especially if there is plenty of room for growth for present employees.

There are times when a company's immediate needs are pressing and there is not time to develop people for promotion internally. In other instances, you may need someone with a certain expertise that does not exist among current employees. Both of these situations demand that you seek candidates from the outside.

Whether you promote or transfer an employee from within

the company or recruit someone from the outside, you would do well to utilize the Profile and Evaluation process to select your winner from among a number of candidates.

The World Is Your Oyster

Networking is probably the primary source of finding top people without paying recruitment fees. Many of the sources listed in Chapter 6 depend, for their full utilization, upon your skill at networking.

Networking is a system of meeting and keeping in touch with a variety of people within your industry and related areas. It is a way to know your competitors and your customers and to find potential candidates who may fill positions within your company. The idea is to build up a broad network of names you can go back to at any time, either to find candidates or to ask for recommendations.

Networking gives you the opportunity to keep in touch with people you have seen in action and who have impressed you. A good example of this can be found at conventions or trade shows. The technical or sales representatives at the display booths are well worth observing. When you see people within your own industry who exhibit qualities you admire, get their names and add them to your network file. When an opening occurs, you can contact these people, either as potential candidates or as sources of referrals. It is a truism that good people generally flock together. Good people tend to know other good people in their industry or associated industries. Getting referrals from them will increase your odds of hiring winners.

Networking makes good business sense on many fronts. It is a valuable source that costs you very little. It can provide contacts, as in the example above, and it can help you keep informed of new trends in your industry. Networking can also enhance your relationships with former and current customers and even help you come up with solutions to problems common to your business.

In terms of recruitment, where the focus is on your personal needs, you should make your needs known to a broad base of people. The more people you know and maintain contact with, the greater your resources.

It is extremely important to instill in all key employees a networking consciousness. One method to encourage this is to develop a reward system. At the end of each quarter, for instance, the person with the greatest number of referrals placed in the skills bank could be rewarded in some way. Keep in mind that these are not referrals of candidates but referrals of contacts for your networking system.

Every time employees attend a seminar, trade show, or convention and meet and interact with other people, they should return with the names of people they have met. Each name should be accompanied by a notation as to how that person might be effective in helping the company find people in the future. If top management insists that this function be part and parcel of the performance measurement of key staff members, this automatically creates a functioning networking system.

Opportunity Hiring

Not all hires originate as a result of a planned recruitment effort. Sometimes opportunity knocks when you least expect it.

- Perhaps there is a defection of personnel from a direct competitor. Several key people unexpectedly apply to your company for employment.
- Perhaps one of your colleagues meets an extremely talented person at a trade show. This person has the capability of taking the company into areas that it contemplated entering a few years down the line.
- Perhaps someone you have known personally recently lost her job. You have long admired her ability to make things happen. Although she has been in an entirely different industry, you think she could become a major asset to your company.

What kind of action should you take?

First, you must base your decision upon sound business

reasons. Can the company afford to add personnel at this time? On the other hand, can it afford not to take advantage of this possible opportunity hire? These decisions require analysis and consultation.

Suppose the company determines that it is a good business decision to consider the hire(s). How, then, would you apply the PIE System?

To start, you must construct a Profile.

Begin with the performance expectations: If you hired this person, what specific, measurable results would you expect by the end of the first year? (You can also divide these results into quarterly achievements.) Follow what you have learned in earlier chapters.

From your list of performance expectations, develop the success patterns and personal characteristics that would be required to meet these expectations. Try not to let the experiences and background of the candidate influence these requirements. It's your job to create a list to which you can compare your candidate *objectively*.

If time permits (that is, if the candidate does not need an immediate response), try to find other candidates for comparison. This is usually more difficult for "opportunity hires," as you have not really conducted a recruitment campaign. If you cannot find any viable competitors, it is all the more important that you not skip all the other steps in the PIE System.

Opportunity hires can result in excellent opportunities for a company. However, they must be carefully considered and evaluated from two aspects: Is it a sound business decision to take on another employee, and if it is, is this the right person to hire?

Your Source Bank

Earlier in this chapter, under "Looking Within," we referred to a skills bank of talent made up of current employees. Another "bank" that needs to be established will likely become your major source for locating candidates. Let's refer to this as your source bank.

Data that go into your source bank may originate from unsolicited résumés and applications or from names and information gathered by your employees in networking.

To develop a source bank, you first need to determine what professional disciplines the company requires on a fairly continuous basis. For example, a small manufacturing company that has minimal hiring needs may define four basic disciplines:

1. Administration and finance
2. Sales and marketing
3. Production
4. Engineering

On the other hand, a growing high-technology company that is always in short supply of good people may have an extensive list of categories in fairly narrow disciplines. In engineering alone, it may have five to ten subcategories. By the same token, a company that has a need for mechanical engineers could subdivide its source list within this category. Another company may have subdivisions for college graduates with a theoretical background, for practical people who have developed products, and for highly educated scientific people. However, you should beware of overcategorization because it can cause you to miss people. If you narrow your focus down to a very small field, you will miss many of the candidates and sources available to you.

The purpose of establishing categories is to provide a means for retrieving names and data when a new personnel requirement presents itself. The system you use to do this file sourcing may be as simple as reading the résumés and notes that are alphabetized in the appropriate category files or as sophisticated as retrieving the information from an elaborate computer database.

Every time someone submits a résumé or application to the company or when a staff member returns from a conference with a contact name, the data should be entered in the source bank. A procedure requiring employees to complete a Source Bank Input Form each time they attend a seminar or conference can make a significant contribution to the source bank. This form should relate as much as the employee knows about the source, including where the person might fit within the company or what type of person this individual might be able to refer to the company.

When staff members return from conferences and other meetings with business cards of people they have met, they can put them in a central Rolodex file. If they file cards under a person's name, they should cross-reference them to type of industry and the name of the individual's company. When you have a specific company in mind as a potential source of good candidates, you have a lead at your fingertips.

Even if your company is large enough to have a personnel department, it is still wise for all other departments to have the capability to define their own source list. Nobody knows better than the managers what type of people they need.

To develop a strong source bank, top management needs to motivate all employees to participate. Whether it is a technician going to a training program, a secretary going to a seminar, or a vice-president going to a national convention, everyone should have a responsibility to network and contribute to the source bank. If people realize that one of the criteria their performance will be judged on is networking and developing a source list, they will indeed contribute to this important function.

Part of the employee selection process should involve keeping track of good sources. Which have been the most fruitful?

If you have hired people from a local junior college, maintain good contacts with the professors and the placement office there. If you have had less success recruiting at a high-powered, sophisticated college (perhaps your business is more nuts-and-bolts practical), you might decide not to waste time pursuing candidates at that school. The same holds true for various kinds of companies: Some may be good sources, others may be useless. You learn these things through experience, and you only remember them if you make note of them.

Never waste a resource. Even if someone who submitted an application or résumé to your company is plainly unsuitable for employment, he or she may know of someone who is ideal. A networking consciousness should become a part of a company's operating basis and be instilled in all employees. It is well worth the effort.

Finally, someone needs to have the responsibility of synthesizing all the information that is gathered and placing it into a system that can be used for retrieval later. Human resources departments often do this job, but in smaller companies a secretary or administrative assistant is often assigned to be the focal point for this data.

Seek and Ye Shall Find

The search for a candidate begins by establishing who in the company should be responsible for achieving the desired result—that is, hiring a winner. There are basically three choices. The search can be directed *and/or* conducted by the human resources department, by a specially assigned executive, or by the president. Some of the considerations that go into selecting the lead person are availability of time, accessibility to sources and candidates, capability, confidentiality (the president might not want others to learn about certan contemplated changes), and ability to attract potential candidates.

A distinction should be made between the words *directed* and *conducted*. A directed recruitment effort is managed by one person with someone else actually doing the initial sourcing and interviewing. Someone within the firm *must* direct the recruitment effort. That person will either conduct the recruitment effort or have someone else—another employee or an outside firm—do all or part of the work. A conducted effort, on the other hand, means that one person handles the complete recruitment effort.

The next chapter describes many of the sources available, including employment agencies, recruitment firms, executive search firms, research firms, and other consultants.

Keep in mind, however, that learning how to apply the PIE System will enable you to select winners as successfully as, if not better than, professional recruiters. Time and confidentiality and other factors may still present problems and force you to have an outside company conduct the search, but even if you need to do that, the PIE System will help you control the associated risks.

6

Sources

The real key to all search is networking. The sources in this chapter form a good foundation on which to build your recruiting program. Ultimately, however, it becomes a numbers game: The more people you talk to, the better your chances of coming up with a potential winner. For when you have gathered several potential winners from which to choose, it is virtually certain that by the end of the process you will have *the* winner you need.

How to Find Winners

Following, in alphabetical order, is a list of methods and sources to help you find winners.

Advertising

Institutional advertising in newspapers and trade magazines— or even on billboards—lets people know your company exists. You may list some positions you are always seeking to fill or just relate that you are an exciting employer. These advertisements should be placed on a continual basis, such as weekly or monthly. They reinforce the image of your company as an aggressive employer with many rewarding career opportunities.

Specific advertising in newspapers and trade magazines seeks candidates for a particular job. Describe your company, the qualifications required in candidates, and the results you seek to achieve. *Use the Profile as a guide when writing the ad.* The most economical/effective advertising days for newspapers are Sundays and Mondays. Ask the ad salespeople if they have special contract rates for companies, discounts based on the number of times an ad appears, or any other special deals. Don't be afraid of using "white" space around your ad, or large headlines, or anything else to make it stand out.

Alumni Placement Offices

Most universities have an active alumni placement office. The résumés of alumni who seek changes in their careers are often on file there. Generally, someone from the company will have to go to their office and review books of résumés. There is no charge for this service, and the office staff is usually helpful.

Associations

Most trade and professional associations have a central clearing-house or committee for members who wish to change jobs. Members send their résumés to the chairman in the hope that inquiries will be generated. These chairmen can quickly tell you who might be available and will often direct you to others who may be able to recommend candidates. Association meetings and publications, of course, are other potential sources.

A source for finding trade and professional associations is the *National Trade and Professional Associations of the United States,* published by:

> Columbia Books, Inc.
> 1350 New York Avenue, N.W.
> Suite 207
> Washington, DC 20005
> (202) 737-3777

The 1990 edition cost $55 and included indexes by association name and subject. Check also with your library for other directories that may provide similar information.

Bankers

If you know any bankers personally (as you should for many business reasons), let them know when you are seeking professional people. Bankers have many contacts in the community and may be able to pass the word around or even refer someone to you.

Bounty Programs

Many companies offer a "bounty" to their employees for referring candidates that are subsequently hired. Bounties may range from $25 to $1,000, depending upon the position to be filled. They are usually paid after the candidate is hired and has been on the payroll for three months.

Bounty programs require a strong kick-off campaign followed by continuous promotion and feedback. For example, one corporation in the early 1960s initiated a bounty program called HOT, an acronym for Hire Outstanding Talent. The company had a logo designed and utilized every opportunity to promote the program, which was most successful among the nonexempt workers and first-level supervisors. The company's middle and upper managers felt a strong, personal need to bring in peers and did so without any bonus incentive.

Good employees generally refer good people, but you must be prepared to tell a referring employee why the person referred was not hired.

Business Articles

Authors of newspaper and magazine articles on business subjects relevant to the position you are seeking to fill can also be sources. For example, if you are looking for a purchasing manager, call the author of an exciting purchasing article and ask for recommendations of candidates. Professionals tend to know other professionals in their field.

Buyer's Guides

In most industries, there is a buyer's guide published to help people find products and services. These guides are also excellent sources of names and titles. An example is a magazine called *HAPPI,* which lists the top fifty companies in the household and personal products industry. Each listing identifies the name of the company, address, phone number, annual sales figures, new products, and other information including the names of the officers and marketing directors. Most industries have similar publications, which can be extremely useful when you are looking for people in a particular industry.

You could call a company and tell the marketing person listed that you are looking for a marketing executive for a particular product. You would describe your company and what you are looking for, then ask for recommendations. You might also ask the person you have called if the job sounds like something of interest to him or her.

College Friends

This source includes fellow sorority or fraternity members, good friends, and even acquaintances you met in school and have kept in touch with. It is particularly effective if your business is in the same locale where you went to school.

College Recruitment

College recruitment is a great source of talent for entry-level professional positions. Both small and large companies recruit new graduates on the campus. It need not be an expensive venture if you concentrate on local schools.

Tell the college placement officers what type of person(s) you want to interview. They will post a notice of your interest and assign a date for your interview.

Unless your company is known in the area, you may get only two or three people to meet with you the first few times. In a brief interview, generally lasting between twenty and thirty minutes, you must decide if you want to spend more time with the candidate at your company.

It is important to sell your company to both students *and* faculty. Send people to the campus who can relate to the students—who, perhaps, are graduates from the school—or whose interests or professional work may relate to some of the faculty. Word spreads quickly. If your company appears to be an exciting one that offers good opportunities, more students will sign up for an interview.

Sometimes faculty members look for summer employment for themselves or for their students. This is a fine opportunity to sell the company by offering meaningful jobs. It should also provide you with some on-campus contacts who can help generate interest in your company and steer the most appropriate students to your interviews.

By the second year (you usually go to the campus twice a year), you will have developed relationships with specific departments and professors who can be a strong source of good people.

Competitors

In any business, it's important to know your competition. This can really pay off in recruitment. You can identify people in competing companies at trade association meetings, through trade publications, and from comments by your customers and vendors. It's easy to send word through the industry grapevine and let people know which position(s) you are trying to fill. Or, if you know who you want, call them directly (see Inquiry Calls in Chapter 8).

Consultants

Many firms use consultants in various aspects of their business. Because consultants work with scores of companies and people, they may be a good source of new employees. (Note that some consultants may charge you a finder's fee, so ask ahead of time.)

Conventions (Also see Trade Shows)

Some people go to conventions and trade shows only to look at products. They do not know that you should also attend these events to look at people. Next time you are at a business, professional, or industry convention, pay attention to the people you meet. When you are given a business card, make a note on the back to remind you of the person and how he or she might help you in the future when you are looking for new employees.

CPA Firms

Accounting firms are a great source of prospects in financial areas. If they are aware that any of their own people want to leave public accounting, they are usually pleased to make the referral. They may also know of people who work for their clients who are looking for a change.

CPA firms do have something to gain by having one of their referrals join your company. If you are already using the firm, it will solidify that relationship. If not, your company may be pleased enough with the referral to begin using the CPA firm.

Customers

Relationships with customers can serve as a network for you to find people. For example, if you are looking for a salesperson, ask the buyers in your customer organizations who the best salespersons are that call on them. If you have a retail store, you might find a new employee who is presently a satisfied customer.

Directories

Directories, such as trade association directories, usually list the names of executives under each company heading. Direct calls to these people can be fruitful. Most people like to give advice. Ask them for help in recommending someone for a particular position.

Directors (Board Members)

Firms that have outside directors on the board should utilize them as a source of employees, particularly for key executives.

Employment Agencies

For a fee, usually paid by the employer, employment agencies refer candidates to companies. Typically, they find candidates by advertising in newspapers, getting referrals from other successful candidates, or interviewing people who simply come to them seeking employment. Generally, agencies handle hourly production people, clerical and secretarial candidates, and beginning-level professional or technical personnel.

They earn their fees by meeting your specifications with one of their applicants and are paid when you hire their applicant. Your company has no commitment unless you hire someone through them. Usually, the employer pays the fee, which is a percentage of the applicant's starting salary. In some instances, the candidate pays the fee, but this is rare.

Fees range from one month's salary to 1 percent for each $1,000 of annual salary up to 30 percent. More often than not, flat percentage deals are cut, say at 20 percent, when the employment agency people feel they can develop a long-term relationship with an employer. As in most other aspects of business, all is negotiable.

Executive Recruiting Firms

Recruiting firms generally handle candidates from the top end of the employment agency range on up through professional people. They attract candidates through advertising, but they also search for candidates who are not necessarily looking to make a job change. They may approach you with candidates whom they feel are appropriate for your company. They will also work on specific recruiting assignments.

Most of their interviews are conducted over the telephone, although they may interview local candidates in person. Their fees, which the employer pays, are 1 percent for each $1,000 of annual salary up to 30 percent, or a flat 20 to 25 percent of annual salary. Fees are open to negotiation.

Recruiting firms may negotiate a retainer, which will be a part of their fee. For the most part, however, they work on a contingency basis, receiving a fee only when you hire one of their candidates. Recruiting firms are often confused with executive search firms (*see* the next classification).

For a directory of executive recruiters (contingency and retainer firms), write to:

> Kennedy Publications
> Templeton Road
> Fitzwilliam, NH 03447

Executive Search Firms

These are the top-level recruiting firms. They seek candidates who are usually professionals, managers, and executives earning in excess of $60,000. Executive search firms work solely on behalf of the employer. Fees usually are 25 to 35 percent of annual compensation, and they are paid even if they are unsuccessful in their quest to find you a candidate. These fees are typically paid in thirds: one-third after thirty days, one-third after sixty days, and the balance upon completion of the engagement. They also receive all expenses associated with the search. A very few search firms charge clients on an hourly basis rather than a percentage of annual salary.

Executive search firms will assist you in the development of a Profile (or something approximating it), conduct research to identify candidates (who are usually employed), travel to interview candidates, check references, and then prepare written reports on the candidates. They will also help in compensation negotiation and any other tasks to make the search successful.

Their work is generally done in the strictest confidence. Companies use executive search firms when: (1) the assignment is to find a replacement for a current executive; (2) public knowledge of who the company wants could be detrimental to the company, such as when entering a new market; or (3) when the company does not have the staff or capability of doing the search itself.

For a directory of executive search consultants, write to:

> Association of Executive Search Consultants
> 151 Railroad Avenue
> Greenwich, CT 06830
> (203) 661-6606

Friends

Friends can be helpful, but they may not understand your business. You may get some unqualified referrals, unemployed relatives of your friends, and, in the process, lose a friend.

Headhunters

Another name for recruiters in recruiting firms and executive search firms.

Human Resources Development Agencies

These are state agencies, the names of which may vary from state to state. These agencies are set up to help out-of-work people find jobs. In an area of high unemployment, they may refer some good leads to you. They do not charge a fee.

Instructors/Professors/Teachers

If you are constantly looking for one type of employee—for instance, plastics engineers—you should form a relationship with an instructor or professor who teaches a course in the subject. If you treat the instructor well (for instance, by offering him or her a summer job), you may develop a friend who will refer the best students to your company.

Interviews

When you interview candidates, ask them to refer people for other positions you may have open. Candidates are usually very cooperative because they hope to impress you with their knowledge and, perhaps, the breadth of their contacts. When you turn down candidates because they do not have the appropriate experience for the job, ask if they know of anyone else. Much depends upon the rapport you have established with these candidates.

Job Fairs

Job fairs bring together a number of companies and hundreds of potential candidates. The job fairs usually have a common denominator, such as technical and engineering personnel or military personnel about to be released from the service.

Each company pays a booth fee, and the organizers promote the fair through advertising and other media events. If you need to hire several people, this can be an economical way to fill your requirements.

Open Houses

Some people are reluctant to send in résumés or take the time to complete an application, even though they may have an interest in, or curiosity about, your firm. Still others do not want to be "screened" by the nontechnical people in the human resources department; they want to discover quickly if a mutual interest exists between them and the people for whom they will be working. This is especially true when there is low unemployment and people have little motivation to look at new jobs.

One way to get prospective employees interested in your company is to hold an open house. At such an event, they can meet directly with the supervisor to whom they would report, if hired. It is less formal than going through the complete selection process, which can be initiated after a person has decided that your company is a good place to work.

Open houses are generally conducted in the evening or on weekends. They can be publicized in newspaper ads that list some of the major recruitment categories of current interest. All employees should be informed of the open house and invited to bring friends who may have an interest in working for the company. Many corporations hold open houses at regular intervals, depending on their recruitment needs.

Outdoor Advertising

Some companies place advertisements on billboards along major commuting routes. These are usually institutional ads, but they can also advertise an open house.

Outplacement Firms

When outplacement firms first became an industry, their primary activity was to help "displaced" executives get over the psychological effects of having been fired as well as to help them find new jobs. Today, outplacement firms work in all types of situations where employees need to find another job.

Many excellent people have found themselves unemployed because of mergers, acquisitions, and restructurings. You may contact outplacement firms and advise them of your requirements. They will place you on their mailing list so that you can find out whom they have available. There is no fee associated with the service.

For a directory of outplacement firms write to:

> Kennedy Publications
> Templeton Road
> Fitzwilliam, NH 03447

Patent Libraries

The local patent library is an excellent source for finding the names of innovative technical people. You need to identify the classifications of the patents you wish to review. Librarians in the patent offices are usually most helpful.

When you find the patents that appear to be in the area of technology in which you are interested, you will see the names of the company and persons who have submitted the patent. (Keep in mind that it may take several years for a patent to be registered, and thus the names on the patent reflect people employed three or more years ago.) The next step is to call these people and ask them for recommendations of people you could contact. They may volunteer themselves as candidates.

Recent Hires

New employees like to put their best foot forward from the start. Take advantage of this during the orientation/training period and ask them about others who may have an interest in working for the company. Smart companies often have a form that all new employees fill out at the time of hire. This form asks for referrals for some standard positions the company is usually seeking to fill.

References

The names you receive from candidates as business references may serve as a source of additional candidates in three ways.

First, when you speak with the references about the candidate, you can mention that you are looking for several people like the candidate and ask them for other names. Second, if you have established good rapport, you can go back to them at a later date when you have a new requirement. And third, you may find that some reference people themselves may have an interest in a new position. All you need to do is ask.

Research Firms

A new breed of service has emerged in recent years—the search research firm. Initially formed to provide research services to executive search firms, these firms now offer their services directly to hiring companies. They are paid an hourly rate of $50 to $100, with their total fees amounting to about one-fourth to one-third of an executive search fee. As their name implies, they will find candidates via the telephone and provide you with a list of names or "minirésumés" of likely prospects. They do not interview any candidates. You are expected to take the next step and contact candidates you are interested in.

For a directory of research firms, write to:

> The Executive Search Research Directory
> Kenneth J. Cole, Publisher
> P.O. Box 9433
> Panama City Beach, FL 32407

Seminars

You probably receive many seminar announcements each month. Don't throw any away without first reading them carefully; they can be a great source of candidates. For instance, the speakers are identified by name and company. If their experience is in the field where you want to hire someone, call them for a referral. They are continually making presentations to groups and should have a solid network of contacts.

When you attend a seminar, meet as many people as possible. Make a note on the back of the business cards you collect or on the attendance list that you can refer to in future. All this expands your network of sources.

Shared Jobs

A recently developed employment concept is to hire two people to share one position. For one reason or another, many talented people in the labor market are not able to commit to an eight-hour-a-day job. Parents who want to be home half-days with their children, students who can only devote part-time to work, retirees, and others with similar needs pose a unique opportunity.

Take two bright people, have each work four-and-a-quarter hours (allow at least a quarter-hour overlap), and give them the Profile of the results you expect to achieve. You may develop a winning combination and fill some difficult job openings.

Summer Hires

Many companies make it a practice to employ additional people for the summer. It's an excellent opportunity to hire college students and to evaluate them for future full-time employment, at the same time showing them what your company is all about.

The experience these summer workers have at your company, whether positive or negative, will be shared with other students. This snowball effect can be instrumental in attracting others from the same school. You need to plan the assignment to make sure it is meaningful.

Temporary Employment Agencies

Temporary agencies offer employees on a daily, weekly, or monthly basis or for the duration of a specific project. Their scope of talent includes production and assembly personnel, clerical and secretarial assistance, and many professionals such as bookkeepers and data processing personnel. There is also emerging a new business geared to providing executives for temporary positions. Watch your newspaper for announcements.

Companies can use the employment of a temporary hire to screen someone they may wish to hire on a permanent basis. Most temporary agencies will negotiate a fee or require a person to be on their payroll for a period such as six weeks before they approve your hiring them full-time. You should let the agency know ahead of time that you want to look at candidates who would be interested in full-time employment.

Trade Shows

There are trade shows for almost every industry, and in some industries there are several shows a year. Here, as mentioned earlier, is a good place to network. Meet as many people as you can, note what they do, and organize your notes when you return to the office.

Trade shows offer a wealth of candidates if you are looking for salespeople. This is an opportunity to see salespeople in action and listen to their booth presentations. If you find people you like, follow through with telephone calls to solicit recommendations and, perhaps, see if they are interested themselves.

Remember, the more people you talk to, the more candidates you will find. It takes time and energy, but the result will be not one but a number of winners from which to select.

Your next step is crucial. It is also one of the most common areas of weakness: The Interview.

7

PIE With EEO on Top

Before you interview a single candidate, you must have at least some basic knowledge of equal employment opportunity (EEO) and other laws that affect the hiring process. This chapter briefly notes some key pieces of legislation and offers general guidelines to help you avoid legal problems. It does *not* attempt to give detailed information on the laws mentioned, which are complex and would require discussion far beyond the scope of this book. Professional counsel should be sought to make sure your company's policies and practices are in compliance with the law.

It's the Law

EEO laws and regulations were established to ensure that every person in the United States has an equal right to obtain employment. Consequently, everyone engaged in hiring activities needs to become familiar with these regulations and, perhaps even more importantly, understand their application and implementation in the employment process.

The Federal Civil Rights Act of 1964, under Title VII—Equal Employment Opportunity, states that is an unlawful employment practice for an employer to discriminate because of a person's *race, color, religion, sex, or national origin*. The law covers actions to hire, discharge, or discriminate against any individual with respect to compensation or terms, conditions, or privileges of employment. The employer must also ensure that any referrals of employees from outside sources, such as employment agencies or others, do not discriminate.

The Age Discrimination in Employment Act of 1967 adds *age* to the above list of areas where discrimination is unlawful. The law's effect is limited to individuals who are at least forty years of age. Discriminatory hiring practices for the *qualified handicapped* are prohibited by the Rehabilitation Act of 1973, and the Pregnancy Act of 1978 states that a woman may not be treated differently because she is pregnant. (Pregnancy is considered a temporary condition.)

If your company does business with the federal government, there is an additional overlay of requirements under the general heading of affirmative action. This involves the commitment to hire and promote a number of protected minorities within your company in proportion to the geographical proportion of such minorities in your area.

Another area of compliance exists at the state level. Most states have their own set of laws and regulations, which may impose additional regulations for a company to follow.

Two recent pieces of federal legislation with which you should be familiar are the Immigration Reform and Control Act of 1986 and the Americans with Disabilities Act of 1990. The first requires employers to certify that all employees hired after November 6, 1986, are eligible to work in the United States. The second prohibits employers from discriminating against disabled employees or job candidates. More than 1,000 "disabilities" are covered by the Act, including impaired sight and hearing, AIDS, depression, diabetes, and epilepsy.

The following general guide should be helpful in your employment process while supporting and complying with the EEO laws and regulations. Please remember that it is not a substitute for professional legal advice.

What does EEO compliance mean to you? What actions should you take to ensure that you do not violate any laws against discrimination? If your company has less than fifteen employees *and* expects to remain that size, it is exempt from these laws. For all other companies, though, these laws have changed the way they conduct business.

In many ways, these laws have forced businesspeople to

review some terribly overlooked and underutilized sources of candidates, and in fact many of the people covered by these laws have become major contributors in the business world. One only has to look at the significant role women have taken in many sectors of business and government to see the results of this "minority" over the past decade.

EEO laws apply to *all* aspects of the employment process. In connection with recruitment and hiring practices, this includes, but is not limited to:

1. What you say or don't say in employment ads
2. What questions you ask on your employment application
3. What questions you should not ask in an interview
4. What your responsibilities are in working with outside recruitment sources
5. How you structure a compensation package
6. How you develop job requirements

In this chapter, you will see how the PIE Selection System actually assists you in complying with EEO regulations.

Let the World Know

Corporate policy comes from the top—the president. An EEO policy statement originates in your "oval office" and must be established and practiced by all employees. Appropriate guidelines need to be developed, communicated, implemented, and adhered to. Either a key executive or a human resources professional should be the implementor.

The company's EEO policy must also be communicated to all outside agencies and firms that provide employees to your company. This would include employment agencies, recruitment firms, executive search firms, colleges, and in fact all of the other sources identified in Chapter 6. The policy statement could be as brief: "We are an equal employment opportunity company. We expect you to provide candidates to us without discrimination or prejudice as to race, creed, color, sex, religion, national origin, age, or handicap."

Your local EEO office will have a full range of information for you, including appropriate signs/posters to be displayed.

The Profile Is Once Again Basic

EEO guidelines stress the importance of ensuring that the job requirements developed for a position are truly based on valid needs to perform the job. One example is the number of years of experience needed to be considered for the position. EEO regulators would argue that you must be able to defend the position that "five to eight years of experience is required" when someone with four years is not acceptable. The success patterns inherent in developing the Profile are based on experiences and accomplishments rather than years of experience. Your defense for the need for such experience and accomplishments is your performance expectations, which are realistic, anticipated results.

The same should be true of the personal characteristics, which must be created from valid requirements of the performance expectations. Although more subjective and at times difficult to determine in a candidate, nevertheless, the expectations should not be discriminatory according to EEO guidelines.

In the Profile, with its use of absolutes and pluses, some requirements are a must (the absolutes) while others are desirable (the pluses). To be in compliance with EEO, you would need to be able to show why the absolutes are in fact absolute requirements. Again, based on your performance expectations, this should be a logical conclusion. A particular technical degree may be an absolute for a particular technical position, and "completed a college degree" may only be a desirable accomplishment (a plus) for still another position. In the latter case, then, a qualified applicant might substitute experience or other accomplishments for the degree.

If your employment advertising adheres to the success patterns, compliance should be virtually automatic. Naturally, you do not indicate in your ad copy any suggestion that a particular sex or age group is more or less desirable than another—*unless* you can prove that such discrimination is not arbitrary. For instance, federal law allows age discrimination in employing police officers, airline pilots, and other specialists who contend with physical demands on the job. By the same token, it would be difficult to prove that most professional and managerial positions have any similar blanket selection criteria.

Compliance Interviewing

"When did you graduate from high school?" (*What year did you reach your eighteenth birthday?*)
"Where did you grow up?" (*Were you born in this country?*)
"Are you married?" (*Could your spouse's career cause a move?*)

Any one of the above questions could get you in trouble. It is not so much the question itself, but what you do with the answer. It would be hard to ignore the answer to the third question if you were interviewing a woman candidate for a significant position, and there was a chance that her husband's career could result in a family relocation. However, your decision not to hire her, based on the answer to that question, would be in violation of the EEO laws.

Perhaps as significant, if you did not hire her for other valid reasons but had asked the same question, you might be accused of discrimination. Therefore, DO NOT ASK ANY QUESTIONS THAT COULD BE DISCRIMINATORY!

One more point: If any candidates volunteer information, such as their age or marital status, without your asking the question, that's acceptable. But don't make a point of writing the answer down. In fact, ignore the answer, and do not let it affect your hiring decision. As the judge tells the jury, "Please ignore that last statement." That's asking a lot from human beings, but it's the law.

If you conduct an interview based on a chronological sequence from the "beginning," and if you use the prompts and techniques for probing as we will discuss in detail in the following chapters, you should be able to keep out of trouble.

"Please begin by telling me about your education. From there we'll move on through your career."

"Where would you like me to begin?"

"Start with high school. What did you enjoy in high school? In what courses did you excel? What would you have done differently if you had the opportunity of going through high school again?"

The majority of the candidates you will interview for professional and managerial positions will be most cooperative during the course of the interview. If you inadvertently ask a question that could be considered discriminatory, nothing will probably come of it. But do try to avoid asking such questions. And do not use the information you gathered from that question in forming your decision whether or not to hire the person.

There may be instances where you will run across a candidate who has been very frustrated by his or her efforts to locate a suitable position. If this person belongs to any group that is covered by the EEO regulations, any mistakes in the questions you ask may cause you a problem. If you decide not to hire this person, even if you base your decision on the objective requirements contained in the Profile, the rejected applicant may file a claim of discrimination. This could result in costly litigation for you and your company. It just makes good business sense to not ask any questions which may be interpreted as discriminatory.

EEO in Evaluation

You will learn in Chapter 14 about the construction and use of a Candidate Evaluation Form. For now, suffice it to say that the form is based on the success patterns and personal characteristics discovered during the interview.

In evaluating candidates, compare each person to the Profile and then to each other. The factors measured are as objective and non-EEO-discriminatory as the success patterns and the personal characteristics you have developed. If the candidate is evaluated properly, the measurement is based on valid job requirement criteria—a hard measure to be disputed by a candidate, the EEO, or anyone else.

The same statement applies to checking references. Here you take the non-EEO-discriminatory success patterns and personal characteristics you uncovered during the interview and verify them with people who should be able to judge firsthand if your assessment was accurate. Again, these are objective measures.

The main thing to remember—and remember well—is to know your laws and to avoid anything that can be construed as discriminatory.

8

Get Ready . . .

Why do you interview candidates? This simple question has an obvious, simple answer: To find out if they are suitable for the position. But interviewing, like quicksand, can be treacherous. If you step off the correct path, you can be up to your neck in problems.

A shocking number of managers try to travel this path without a map and end up in the quicksand. Not trained to interview thoroughly, many do not understand what they need to learn from the interview. They merely check a candidate's résumé, ask a few short questions, and generally try to get the process over with as quickly as possible. By failing to get the most out of an interview, these managers shortchange both the candidate and the company.

Interviewing is a skill that can be learned by anyone with the willingness to learn. It is also sometimes considered an art, but that elevated status comes only after extensive experience.

There are two key questions in interviewing: (1) How do you discover if a candidate is capable of meeting your requirements, and (2) what exactly do you want to discover? It is in these important points that the interview process often fails.

In the PIE System, the basic premise of interviewing is that candidates will typically perform in the future as they have in the past. When you find out *what* candidates have accomplished in the past and *how* they have done so, you have a strong indication of how they will work for you in the future. This is how you find the real winners.

This doesn't preclude exceptions or the fact that some people can change. Generally, however, if you find people who have proven themselves to be intelligent, ambitious, and productive through impressive prior accomplishments, the chances are they will continue this behavior in the future. They represent the type of person you should look for in order to reduce your hiring risks.

In interviewing candidates for important positions, you must go beyond the résumés and application forms and what you may have heard about the individuals from your sources. You need to delve deeply into their backgrounds to get a first-hand picture of who they are, what they've accomplished, and what they think they are going to do in the future. *You must then accurately evaluate this information against your needs.*

The best way to do this effectively is to utilize the Profile as a basis for discovery, if you will, of what the people are all about and how they will contribute to, and fit into, your company. Without the Profile, the interview would simply consist of conversation. With the Profile, the interview is directed at discovering how each candidate fits the job specifications. Here is where you look for success patterns and personal characteristics.

Be Prepared

Today's job candidates are better prepared for interviews than ever before. Look in any bookstore and you'll see a dozen books on writing résumés, on dressing well, on how to impress interviewers. Many candidates don't even write their own résumés anymore—they hire professionals. There are also many courses available to teach candidates job-hunting skills and prepare them for interviews.

You need to be as well prepared as the candidates!

Your first step in preparing for an interview is to study the Profile. Everyone interviewing the candidates should know the desired success patterns and personal characteristics. They form the path to discovery during the interview. The next step is to review each individual's résumé and/or application. Do so with a cool eye. A study by one California executive search firm claims that 45 percent of all applicants lie about their salaries, job responsibilities, or past accomplishments. Up to 30 percent lie about their educational degrees. My own experience does not bear out these figures. I have found that only a very small percentage of candidates lie outright; they are more likely to exaggerate facts and to omit data that might be harmful to them.

One fact can be taken as a given: A résumé will show you what the candidate wants you to know. In all cases, candidates will try to present their best side. This is not unethical; it's the way the game has come to be played.

Buyer Beware!

Some résumés contain what I call red flags—obvious inconsistencies that scream out a warning. All résumés have some yellow caution flags—areas where it would be wise for you to dig a little deeper. Your job is to go through the résumé to look for inconsistencies and anything else that is waving a yellow flag at you. You must probe these areas during the interview.

There are certain things you want to watch for. For example, when the résumé states that the person left a job in 1987 and started another job in 1988, you want to find out the length of time between jobs. In actuality, there could almost be a two-year gap if the employee left in January 1987 and started the new job in December 1988. I once discovered that a person had had three jobs in between the two listed on his résumé.

By having a candidate account for all the time between jobs, you learn something about that candidate's stability or instability.

It is also important to find out whether job changes signaled an upward progression. Did the applicant's responsibilities increase? Did compensation increase? Or has the candidate been stagnant or moving backward in the last few jobs? Find out the true trend.

Many people briefly describe the duties and responsibilities of a job on their résumés. You need to go beyond these words to find out what, in fact, they actually did. "Responsible for all the financial affairs of the company" tells you very little about a chief financial officer. Was she active in raising capital? Did she put in a computer system? Did she have any effect on cost controls?

The trend today is for candidates to put accomplishments on their résumés: "During my three years with the company sales went from $10 million to $25 million." Great, but was he instrumental in achieving the increase? Or was it simply because the company had a monopoly on the product and sales would have risen no matter who was in charge? It's very important that you understand exactly what the candidates have accomplished. Their résumés will not tell you all you need to know. You must ask.

Other areas to look at include ambiguous statements and/or claims. For instance, there are ways to imply that one has a degree without exactly lying. The candidate might put down "M.B.A. Program." A quick glance would lead you to believe that she has an M.B.A. In fact, she only attended the MBA program. Another candidate might list Harvard Business School under Education, which again leads you to think that he received a degree from Harvard. In fact, he attended a twelve-week program there. There's nothing wrong with a twelve-week program—unless you mistake it for a full two-year advanced degree.

You can either mark these yellow flags with notes directly on the résumé or make a separate list of them. The point is to keep track of them in a form you can use during the interview. Many will be answered naturally during the interview as it progresses. At the end of the interview, check your notes to make sure that all your points have been covered.

An Alpha Applicant

Chapter 4 presented a Profile for a regional sales manager needed by the Alpha Corporation. Now we have an applicant, a person by the name of George W. Spencer. Let's take a close look at his résumé (Figure 2) and see if he is indeed a viable candidate.

If you refer to the Profile we developed for Alpha in Chapter 4, page 40, it seems that George Spencer is a strong

Figure 2. George Spencer's résumé.

RÉSUMÉ

George W. Spencer   *Res: (408) 555-1234*
468 N. Camino Blvd.,   *Bus: (408) 555-5678*
Cupertino, CA 94535

OBJECTIVE: A senior sales or marketing position with a fast-growing
company in the computer or systems business.

EXPERIENCE:

1984–Present FINANCIAL MANAGEMENT SYSTEMS (FMS),
              Sunnyvale, CA
              REGIONAL SALES MANAGER, N. California
              • Managed three technical salespersons, producing
                revenues of over $2 million in 1988
              • Negotiated major contracts with several retail chains
              • Hired and developed a strong sales support team
              • Received the President's Award for being the #1 sales
                person in both 1985 and 1986

1982–1984   BROWARD PUBLICATIONS, Textbook Division,
              Chicago, IL
              MAJOR ACCOUNT MANAGER
              • Obtained largest textbook sale in company's history
              • Represented the company at national trade shows
              • Achieved sales of over $1 million the first year

1977–1981   ZERON CORPORATION, Chicago Branch, Chicago, IL
              FIELD SALESPERSON
              • Specialized in a/v sales to schools and universities in
                the Greater Chicago area
              • Always ranked among the top three salespersons
                within the company
              • Received "Rookie of the Year" Award, 1978

EDUCATION:
    BS Business Administration, University of Wisconsin, 1977
        Major in Marketing and Finance
    MBA Program, Loyola University, Chicago, 1979
        Additional courses in advanced sales techniques.

PERSONAL:
    Married. Home Owner. Enjoy tennis and jogging.
    References available upon request.

candidate. Let's look at his résumé closely, however, keeping the success patterns of the Profile in mind.

Critique of George Spencer's Résumé

Are There Unaccountable Time Gaps?

A cursory review of the résumé indicates that Mr. Spencer moved directly from one job to the next. However, we don't really know for sure. He states that he left Zeron in 1981 and joined Broward in 1982. The question is, When in 1981 did he leave Zeron and when in 1982 did he join Broward? There could be a significant time gap here. Is he hiding a short-term position with another employer?

The same holds true for his move from Broward to FMS in 1984. We need to find out exactly when the move took place.

Can We Follow a Logical Career Progression?

Mr. Spencer progressed from field salesperson to major account manager to regional sales manager. This appears a reasonable progression of responsibilities. What we need to probe is why he is interested in the Alpha regional sales manager position. Would it be a real step forward for his career?

Is There a Pattern of Short-Term (Less Than Two Years) Jobs?

Unless there are other jobs during periods of unaccountable time, he appears to have had a fairly stable career.

Are There Success Patterns That Coincide With the Profile?

Success Pattern: Have a track record of personally generating sales of at least $2 million annually.

Mr. Spencer indicates that he managed three technical salespersons, producing revenues of over $2 million in 1988. The question is whether he personally produced the sales or whether he just managed the effort. This needs to be explored, as do the sales levels in his previous positions.

Success Pattern: Experienced in selling computer systems to end-user organizations.

It appears that Mr. Spencer is currently selling computer systems to end-users in his position with FMS.

Success Pattern: Experienced selling sophisticated equipment to universities and colleges.

In his sales position with Zeron, Mr. Spencer sold audio/visual equipment to academic institutions. The question may be, Is this sophisticated enough?

Success Pattern: Have a track record of developing new accounts.

One would be surprised if an award-winning salesperson made all his sales to existing accounts. He must have developed new accounts. But to what extent?

Success Pattern: Completed a college degree.

He states he completed a degree. This must be verified.

Success Pattern: Experienced in solving customer problems and establishing solid customer relations.

This may be assumed, but it is not substantiated on the résumé. This would be a good point to check with former customers whom he may list as references.

Which Absolute Success Patterns Are Not Obvious on the Résumé?

Perhaps the only one is the first, referring to personal sales of at least $2 million.

Does the Résumé Specify Results/Accomplishments, or Are the Positions Just Described in General Terms?

The résumé indicates specific results.

Does the Overall Picture Hang Together?

Yes.

Additional Conclusions We May Draw From the Résumé, but
Which Need to Be Confirmed During
the Interview and Reference Checking Procedure:

The objective seems to be in line with career experience and progression and with Alpha's requirements for a regional sales manager.

Did he complete the MBA program? Was this an evening program? Why was he pursuing it?

Tennis and jogging may indicate someone who is active, social, and physically in good shape. It may also indicate a competitive nature.

Married, a home owner, he gives the impression of stability.

All in all, George Spencer seems well worth calling in for an interview. The success patterns we are looking for apparently exist. There are, however, questions that need to be asked, assumptions that need to be clarified, and facts that need to be confirmed. You should cover all of them thoroughly in the interview; you may touch upon some during the first telephone screening.

Inquiry Calls

By utilizing your Profile and contacting sources culled from your source bank and the list in Chapter 6, you should be able to gather a good selection of candidates from which to choose your winner. You are, in effect, doing exactly what professional search firms do to find candidates.

After you have identified the individuals who either could be candidates or may be in a position to refer candidates, you will want to telephone them for a preliminary conversation. This talk won't have the depth or detail of a personal interview, of course, but it should provide sufficient information to judge whether a prospective candidate is worth pursuing.

If you know the person's home phone number, try to call there. In many instances, however, all you'll have is a business card. You can start your dialogue there and continue at home if it's promising.

Keep a copy of the Profile in front of you, and take notes. You know what you are looking for and can lead the person through this screening interview just as you would in person. On the telephone, however, you would not do an in-depth interview. A telephone interview may run anywhere from 15 minutes to 45 minutes, depending upon how thoroughly you want to screen the potential candidate. When you are talking to candidates across the country, the phone interview will obviously be more extensive because the cost of visiting them or having them visit you is a major expenditure. With local people, on the other hand, you might spend less time screening them and then meet the more promising candidates in person.

You might want to begin your telephone conversation along these lines:

"This is [identify yourself and your company]. You submitted an application to our firm . . ." or "One of our employees met you at a recent conference (trade show, etc.) . . .

"We are currently looking for an individual to join our firm as a [give either the title of the position, if it is self-descriptive, or a one-to-two sentence description]. The purpose of this call is to see if there is someone you could recommend for this position. If you have a few minutes, I could describe what we are looking for."

Most people are curious and flattered that you are asking them for advice. They are usually willing to give you a few minutes of their time.

"We require someone who can [paraphrase the performance expectations from the Profile]. Through your years of experience, are you aware of someone who can accomplish these results?"

You generally get one of three reactions. Some people refuse to help, saying they do not give out names of other people; some people cooperate happily and recommend one or more candidates to you; other people express a personal interest in the position. For any of the latter group whom you've contacted at work, you might ask if it would be more convenient to call them at home in the evening for further discussion.

Even in a long phone call, do not tell them too much about the position requirements (the success patterns and personal characteristics). Tell them enough to whet their appetites but not enough to enable them to feed back to you what you want to hear.

Let's assume that you have four absolutes in terms of success patterns. Your task in this conversation is to see if the person has these absolutes. If not, you will be wasting your time to continue further discussion.

Ask the prospects to describe their backgrounds briefly, and then follow the interview format and techniques described in the next four chapters.

"I'd like to ask you a few questions tonight to see if it makes sense for us to carry this another step further. Why don't you give me a thumbnail sketch of what you've done in life, your chronological history."

Most candidates then ask where you want them to start.

"How about from your education to the present time?"

Candidates will usually begin with college graduation and then give the dates, companies, and titles of jobs they've had— not much more than is already on the résumé.

When the person names a title appropriate to the position you're seeking to fill, you start to probe. "Would you explain that job in a little more detail?" Or, "At that time were you involved with A, B, C, or D?"

"A, B, C, and D" are your absolutes, what you really want to find out about in this conversation. If they are missing, you do not have a viable candidate on the other end of the line. In such a case, you can gracefully bring the conversation to a close.

Toward the end of the call, ask the viable candidates to give you a "ballpark area of compensation to make sure it fits in with our thinking."

Some candidates will send it right back to you: "What compensation are you talking about?"

Your response should be to give them an approximate figure. There's no point in playing games here. If the salary is actually in the $60,000–$70,000 range, state that the compensation is in the sixties. At this point, some candidates will mention that their compensation now exceeds the range offered. You have several choices for a response.

If a person seems to fit your Profile and you would like to

have some further discussion, then you could respond, "Perhaps we do have some flexibility. Let's meet and talk about it."

On the other hand, you could also "test" such a candidate with "Maybe this isn't the right position for you" and see how he responds.

The point is that during the telephone screening you need to do two things: first cover the absolutes, then ensure that the proposed compensation fits the candidate's needs. If everything looks promising, either set up the appointment then or ask the person to call you at the office. Make sure that the candidate will be able to spend three or four hours with you. Your first interview may last an hour and a half, and two other people might need to see the candidate as well.

On many occasions, you will determine by the end of a telephone conversation that the person is not a potential candidate. It is best at that point to explain why he or she is not qualified. Keep your comments to the facts and to job experiences that are missing. Do not offend anyone by describing the personal reasons why you are not interested. Then you can ask for recommendations of other potential candidates.

Conclude the conversation by thanking the individual for his or her time, saying, "Should a more appropriate position arise in the future, I would like to contact you again to determine your interest."

After you have made several inquiry calls and have determined whom you would like to see in person, the next step is to schedule a series of interviews.

9

Get Set . . .

As you well know, an interview is not just sitting down with a candidate and talking. You're there to find out some very specific information. The preparation discussed in the previous chapter is essential. Equally important is where and how you conduct the interview.

The Setting

In choosing your interview site, you need an environment in which the candidate will be comfortable and relaxed and in which there will be a minimum of interruptions.

There are people who try to make interviews intimidating. A few executives have even gone to the extreme of reducing the length of a chair's legs so that the candidate is sitting lower than the interviewer, just to make the scene intimidating. Most candidates are nervous and on their guard. It would be more in your interest to get them relaxed enough so that they open up and allow you to find out what you need to know.

Eliminate, or certainly reduce, any interruptions that will throw off the train of thought. If the interview is in your office, instruct your secretary to hold all calls unless they are emergencies. Do not allow people to walk in during the interview, either.

There are three reasons for such measures. First, you are showing the candidate you care about what is happening. Part of this candidate's future may rest with your company, so the least you can do is show interest and respect. Second, privacy is important because your discussion should not be in a place where it can be overheard by any interested parties. If a candidate feels secure about privacy, it is one less barrier to open and willing communication. Third, the interview is by no means a casual chat. You will be following a firm agenda, so it is important that you not get distracted and lose track of your position.

Sometimes interviews can be conducted effectively in restaurants. Restaurants managers who are oriented to business clients know how to minimize the presence of their help. The candidate may also feel more at ease on neutral ground, so to speak.

The physical environment is important and should be chosen with care. You need a place that is quiet, where there are no bright lights or sun shining in the candidate's eyes, and where you are both comfortable.

In an office interview, try not to sit across a desk or table from the candidate. This usually denotes a superior/subordinate situation. It is best to sit at a 90-degree angle to each other. In other words, if you must sit at a desk, the person should be at the side of the desk, not across from you.

The idea is not to put any physical barriers that might block or filter good communications. You want the interviewees to feel totally comfortable, willing to respond spontaneously and to be themselves, as opposed to telling you what they think you want to hear. This is a firm prerequisite to effective interviewing.

The Interview Agenda

There are various methods of conducting an interview and extracting information from a candidate, some more effective than others. The two most prevalent methods are either to start with current employment and work backward or to start with personal history and education and work forward. The PIE System functions more logically by starting with early life and moving forward.

Tracking success patterns and personal characteristics is easier when candidates relate their histories chronologically from the beginning. People tend to repeat themselves, or at least to repeat the patterns of behavior they develop early in life. By starting at a relatively early point in a person's life, one can more easily spot and follow the success patterns.

In some cases, it is like watching a seed sprout and grow. You can see the beginnings in the school years, for instance, and watch the individuals grow and strengthen through the course of their careers. In other cases, the seed begins to sprout and then, for whatever reasons, withers and never really develops fully.

Before you even begin the interview, decide which areas of the candidate's life you will spend the greatest time on. When talking to younger people, pay more attention to schooling than when talking to seasoned executives. In the case of relatively recent graduates, those school years have probably had the greatest impact upon who they are at this moment.

With experienced professionals, on the other hand, although you still need a chronology of where they were and what they did in their early years, your pursuit of their accomplishments in recent years will be more in depth. In either case, it is still important to track the candidate all the way through and see what patterns emerge.

Another factor in judging where your focus should be is, of course, the pertinence of the candidate's career to the position you are trying to fill. If one-third of a person's career has been involved in activities applicable to the position and two-thirds has been more diverse, you would obviously spend more time on the more relevant period.

Finally, you will also decide ahead of time on which yellow flags to focus your attention.

Once you have completed this preliminary planning, you can set the rest of the interview agenda so that you know exactly what you are going to do. Not only does this give you control of the entire interview process so that you get the most out of your time, but it also ensures that nothing important is going to be left out inadvertently. The agenda usually looks something like this:

1. Make the candidate feel comfortable and at ease.
2. Explain the agenda for the day (timetable).

3. Tell the candidate where you would like her to begin discussing her background.

4. When you are satisfied that you have tracked the success patterns and personal characteristics, review the yellow flags to make sure all your questions have been answered.

5. Make sure the candidate knows what the job entails.

6. Obtain her reaction to the position, including what she feels it offers and what she can contribute.

7. Ask if she has any questions about the company.

8. Discuss compensation. (Sometimes this comes up earlier.)

9. Close the interview.

10. Complete a Candidate Evaluation Form. (This is made a part of the interview agenda because of its importance in completion of the interview process discussed in Chapter 14.)

Each of these steps in the interview agenda will be explained more fully in the chapters that follow, but for the moment you should keep in mind that the above is just a guide. No interview ever goes exactly as planned.

You might also discover during the course of the interview, perhaps very early, that the person you are talking to is in no way a good candidate for the job. Then you have to go through these steps rather quickly but graciously so that you don't waste your time or the candidate's.

Surprises will occur; they always do. By following this agenda as closely as possible, however, you will ensure that everything is covered.

Tracking for Posterity

One of your primary tasks throughout the interview is to keep the candidate talking. After all, you are primarily interested in what the candidate says and how it will match or meet your success patterns and personal characteristics. In order to accomplish this purpose, it is important that you take notes as you go through the interview. Have a pad and pencil ready from the beginning, and when the candidate talks, make notes in whatever style is comfortable to you.

Taking notes is an integral part of the interview process. It also indicates to the candidates that you are sufficiently interested in them to make sure you remember what they say. Sometimes it might even be appropriate to say to a candidate at the beginning of the interview, "I hope you don't mind if I take notes. I talk to a lot of people and I really want to make sure I remember who you are." This also shows your interest.

As you probably remember from your school days, your notes should reflect the main theme, the important points, of what is being said. Some notes may refer to questions that need to be answered later, while other notes comment on events or dates to provide a chronology for you to follow. In the context of an interview, perhaps the most important function of note taking is to identify the success patterns and personal characteristics of the candidate.

Take notes as often as you feel you need to. This differs from person to person. You will, of course, keep the notes to provide the information you need to make an evaluation after the interview.

One important point of caution, however. If something very negative comes up, *do not* quickly make a note. If, for example, the candidate says, "Boy, that was a terrible experience—I got fired because they thought I embezzled something," don't make a note. If you do, thus showing that you find this negative important, it may cause the candidate to freeze or simply to feel cautious or intimidated.

Instead, when something negative comes up, remember the item, and when the candidate next makes a positive statement, record the negative item on your sheet.

Of course, there may be times when you find it impossible to avoid making an issue of a negative at that time. You might have to say to a candidate that something doesn't make sense and that you can't follow it. "I thought you said you were working here and not there at that time."

While your notes should obviously track the success patterns and personal characteristics you are looking for, they should also list any other facts that strike you as important during the interview. If something comes across during the interview that concerns you—perhaps the person really had three jobs in two years when the résumé indicated only one— you should make a note of that. You wouldn't necessarily say anything about the discrepancy at that point, but the note will help you return to it later in the interview.

Your note-taking thus helps you to avoid disrupting a candidate's thought processes. If the conversation is flowing well, you do not want to interrupt with a question or comment; simply make a note to bring it up at a later time.

The point is that you do want to make sure that you follow the chronology and track the person accurately. Whenever possible, make notes and bring these points up later. Done properly and with discretion, note taking simply makes sense.

10

Go . . .

No interviewer can follow by rote an inflexible script; you must be able to adapt to different circumstances as they occur. However, with a workable guide, you have a framework on which to build, and your improvisational skills can thus improve.

What follows is just that, a workable guide. In this chapter, you will find all the techniques and clues to keep a candidate talking . . . and on track. You will learn how to dig into a candidate's answers in order to find out who the person really is under that facade.

If you follow these techniques and use them often enough, you will soon become an excellent interviewer, able to find the information you need to select your winners.

Forget the Rubber Hose

Making the candidates feel comfortable begins with seeing them at the appointed time. People who subscribe to the stress interview theory are inclined to keep candidates waiting in the lobby for twenty or thirty minutes. This is unnecessary, demeaning, and ultimately self-defeating.

All candidates should be made to feel that not only is the job important but also that they are important. Courtesy is the oil that greases the squeaky wheels of society, and the workplace is no exception. A candidate who feels your lack of respect is unlikely to feel respect for the position, the company, or you. It isn't a constructive beginning.

After meeting the candidate on time, take him or her into the room in which the interview will take place and offer the person a seat. If appropriate, suggest coffee or a soft drink.

Then comes a short period of small talk. "Were my directions okay? Did you have trouble finding us?" or whatever seems appropriate. Most people expect these socially acceptable opening comments. It may only be a sentence or two, lasting a few seconds or a minute, and it may seem trite, but it helps the person to settle down and get comfortable.

An earlier statement bears repeating: A comfortable candidate is more likely to open up and be receptive to your questions. It's worth taking the little time and trouble needed to put the candidate at ease. Now you are ready to start the interview.

It's All Talk

Your opening statement should let the candidate know exactly why you are both there. It would be something on the order of: "The purpose of this interview is for us to get better acquainted so that we can understand your capabilities and experience relative to the position we are talking about."

You are now going to begin tracking the candidate's activities. Again, let him know what you are looking for: "I'd like to know as much as I can about you. Perhaps you could start from the beginning. I'd like to know about your schooling, your later education, and then your work history to the present." You are taking the chronological approach from past to present.

You might then start by asking what was significant for the candidate during high school. What did he like and dislike about it, and what did he achieve?

Some candidates will give you a puzzled look at this point. A fifty-year-old might ask what relevance his high school days have on the position he is applying for. Your answer is that you are concerned about his whole life, everything that has led up to what he is today.

During one interview, a candidate said, "What I did more than ten years ago is not significant to this discussion." She virtually told the interviewer that it was none of his business.

"It has nothing to do with my qualifications for this job," she continued. Her activities for the most recent ten years were appropriate to the job, and she was willing to discuss them, but she was quite defensive about discussing anything from an earlier period.

The interviewer accepted this, but it couldn't help but influence his opinions about her communication skills, her eagerness for the job, and her cooperativeness. He also had a concern about whether she was hiding something in her past. Legally, however, he had no right to pursue the issue.

It turned out that after a while, when rapport between the two had been built up, she volunteered the information he was seeking. She had been working in a different profession and in an unrelated industry. He never did find out why she was so reluctant to provide the information in the first place. Her attitude did have an influence on his decision. She ended up being the number-two candidate out of fifteen. Number one took the position.

This was a rare occurrence, however. Most people will be quite willing to cooperate.

Control

Once the interview starts, some candidates will immediately try to take control of the process. You have to stop that right from the beginning. You cannot lose control of the interview, or else you will not find out the information you are seeking.

Suppose the candidate starts by saying, "This is a very interesting company. Why don't you tell me about it?"

Fine, this is a reasonable request. Take five or ten sentences to give a broad view of the company. But if in the next breath the candidate says, "That sounds great. Tell me about the position," you have to put on the brakes and turn the interview around right there.

"I'll be happy to tell you all the details about the position, but first let's go through your background," you say.

It is very important that you control the interview. If you don't, some candidates will start asking you questions. At the end of such an interview, you will know very little about the candidate, and he or she will have all the input. In such interviews, candidates can tailor their responses to your stated needs and tell you exactly what they think you want to hear. For example, suppose you state in responding to a question about the company that "it's a very young, aggressive company, very dynamic, with no barriers, and everyone just charges ahead." I'll guarantee that the smart candidates will soon say or imply that they are aggressive and dynamic, dislike all barriers, and just want to charge ahead.

It's very important that you do not provide leads or clues for the candidates to follow. If you start answering questions instead of asking them, you will lose control of the direction of the interview.

For the most part, you will be dealing with very savvy candidates. They've read the books and taken the courses on how to succeed in an interview. They have learned how to spot the clues and adapt to them. While this may be a skill to be admired, it won't increase your chances of finding a winning candidate.

By following the chronological sequence from the candidates' early years to the present and then moving into their goals for the future, and by sticking closely to this agenda, you will maintain control of your interviews.

Silence Is Golden

Shakespeare decried "the disease of not listening" in *Henry IV*, and it's an illness that has been with us for a very long time. We all know people who never listen, and it is not surprising that sooner or later most people stop talking to them. Needless to say, this is not what we want to happen during an interview.

One of the most important actions an interviewer can take is to listen actively. You have created a setting in which there will be no interruptions because you want the candidates to speak with as few interruptions as possible from you or anyone else. You do not want to derail a candidate's train of thought; you want him or her to keep on talking without wandering too far off the track you have established for the interview.

The temptation to talk, to chase away the silence with a rush of words, is irresistible for most of us. In the interview setting, however, a crucial part of *your* job is to listen. It is the candidate's job to break the silences.

A very successful interview is based on the 80/20 rule. The candidate should talk 80 percent of the time, and you should talk only 20 percent of the time (prior to the point you start telling the candidate about your company). If you follow this rule, you will ask the right questions, probe properly for the answers, and learn all you need to know about the candidate.

If the ratio is reversed, as it often is, you will give away the store. Probably the biggest culprits I've seen in this area are the presidents or sales executives of companies. Naturally enough, they like to talk about themselves, about the company, and about the excitement of the business. In doing this, they learn nothing about the candidate and give all the clues the candidate needs to respond to any questions they may ask.

Candidates also need to feel you are interested in them. After one candidate had an interview with a company executive, she said to me, "You know, we spent two hours together, but he doesn't know anything about me. He spent all the time talking about his company and the situation, and he kept trying to sell me, which was fine, but I'm not sure how interested he was in me."

One manager had a reputation for interrogations in which all that was missing were the bright lights and rubber hoses. Far from establishing any rapport with the candidate, he'd simply bark out questions for fifteen or twenty minutes, barely waiting for any answers before moving on. Candidates' reactions ranged from fear to intense dislike. After some proper training in the skill of interviewing, this manager spent four or five times longer with the candidates and left them feeling that he was truly interested in who they were.

A related rule is never to be judgmental about a candidate's answers or comments. If you disapprove of some method the candidate used to accomplish something, keep it to yourself or you will soon have a silent and/or resistive candidate.

The 80/20 rule ensures not only that you get all the pertinent information but also that the candidate leaves the interview with much more positive feelings than if you violate this rule.

Listening is not passive; in fact, it must be quietly active. Interviewers must *demonstrate* genuine interest and should never show boredom or impatience, judgmental attitudes, or any other negative reactions that would tend to discourage the candidate from talking. Nor should the listening be forced or in any way insincere. Candidates must feel that there is true interest in everything they have to say.

But there is more to keeping a candidate talking than simply listening. To bring this about, we use a number of techniques that we call *prompts,* through which you encourage the person to continue talking.

Open-Ended Questions

Never ask a question that can be answered with either a yes or a no. It is more effective to ask open-ended questions that require some discussion.

A question like "Did you like your last job?" is closed-ended. The one-word answer you're likely to get will tell you very little about the candidate. A better question would be open-ended: "What did you like about your last job?" or "What were your likes and dislikes about your last job?"

When no one-word response is available, the candidate will keep talking and you will get more information.

Open-ended questions usually pose a how, why, and what to the candidate. For instance, don't ask if the candidate was laid off, ask why the candidate left that position.

Further examples of open-ended questions will be given in the next chapter.

The Laundry List

A laundry list is a question that gives the person several items to cover. For example: "Tell me about your education. I would like to know what courses you took, what courses you liked and disliked, and which courses you did best in."

The purpose of a laundry list is to get the candidate to talk in depth, covering several facets of an area. It also allows you to ask a fairly short question and get a much longer answer, once again following the 80/20 rule.

If you are talking to a person about a production management position, for instance, you might say, "Why don't you tell me about how you managed your people. What style of management did you use? How did you motivate and reward your people?" That is a laundry list of questions.

The only danger in using the laundry list is that all your questions may not be answered. You must keep track of exactly what you asked in order to make sure that every item on the list has been covered before you leave the subject.

The Parrot Phrase

This probing tool is named after the bird for a good reason: You are repeating the candidate's statement and then adding a question mark at its end. For instance, if the candidate says, "I really enjoyed setting up the new management information system," you respond, "You really enjoyed setting up the management information system?" The candidate will then tell you why she enjoyed setting up the system, and probably a lot more.

The parrot phrase encourages the candidate to give more depth to a subject. The candidate says, "I didn't like that boss." You say, "You didn't like that boss?" The candidate will then most likely explain to you what the problem was. He senses that you want more details.

Another example: When the candidate says that a company was great to work for, you could respond, "It was great to work for?"

This is the parrot phrase, and it is another effective prompting method.

Body Language

Body language is a system of judging how body posture, gestures, and other movements reveal—or at least give a clue to—

an individual's attitudes. It's an important part of an interview, and you would do well to read a book on body language—as many candidates have. In the meanwhile, however, here are a few basic tips on how to project the right body language.

When you are talking to an individual, sit attentively and look as if you are interested. Lean into the interview, as if you are hanging onto a candidate's words. It is all a part of giving the total appearance that you are truly listening—which, indeed, you should be. This prompts the candidate to keep talking.

Be open, and have gestures that are open. Don't cross your arms, which is a way of saying, "Okay, prove it to me now." These are all signals that come across to a person, consciously and subconsciously.

Maintaining eye contact is another important part of body language. It tends to keep the candidates talking and lets them know that they have your attention.

You'll find that with these and other prompts, you won't have to do much talking.

The Pause That Intimidates

The pause is another way of using silence as a prompt. You will find that when you pause, not saying anything for a length of time after a candidate makes a statement, he or she will start talking again.

The candidate, like most people, cannot stand the silence— a void in which nothing is being said. I've never seen a pause go past ten or fifteen seconds. To the candidates that's like minutes. Silence makes them extremely uncomfortable. Candidates, like nature, abhor a vacuum.

The pause should not be overused. After all, you don't want the candidates to be uncomfortable. But when used selectively, the pause is an effective way to get the candidates to continue talking.

"Uh-Huh" and "Yes"

Another way to give positive feedback to the candidate is to nod or say "uh-huh" and "yes" at the appropriate moments. Again, it shows that you are observing and listening and that you want to get all the information you can.

However, once more, this prompt is not to be overused. Saying "yes" at the wrong point in a conversation will do the exact opposite of what you want: It will jar the candidates and make them stop talking. You want this prompt to be encouraging and attentive.

The Poised Pencil

If you are taking notes throughout the interview—and you should be—you can also use your pencil as a prompt. When you hold your pencil alert and ready to make a note, the candidates will want to give you something to write. This prompt has a similar effect to the pause. So keep your pencil poised as if you are ready to take notes.

These prompts will help you keep the candidate talking 80 percent of the time, which is what you want. They may seem artificial at first, and you may feel clumsy applying them, but as you practice interviewing and practice using prompts and other methods to help the candidate divulge the information you need, you will find that the technique becomes easier to use. Prompting will soon be as natural to you as ordinary speaking or listening.

11

Probing . . . Getting Behind the Facade

An interviewer was handed a résumé by an executive who was applying for a rather significant position. During the course of the interview, every time the interviewer asked a question, the executive replied, "Well, it's on the résumé."

The interviewer grew increasingly puzzled and finally said, "You mean your whole twenty-year career is wrapped up on these two pages?" The executive said somewhat irritably that it was.

"Well," the interviewer said, "if you have nothing else to say, then I guess I have nothing else to ask, so that kind of ends our conversation today."

"Wait a minute!" the executive replied quickly. And so the interviewer finally got him to open up.

It was a rather drastic method, but it worked.

Some people are not used to being interviewed, not used to looking for a job. They are uncomfortable in a job interview, and so you have to loosen them up. Sometimes you have to resort to a little shock treatment, as in the previous example. When the interviewer said, in effect, "Fine, thanks, goodbye," the applicant panicked at being cut off so quickly.

Shock treatment is not a method of getting information from a candidate that you should try too often.

Different candidates react to questions in many different ways. There are reticent speakers and verbose speakers. Some speakers try never to answer a question directly, while other speakers tell you more than you'd ever want to know. There are those who lie and those who embellish, those who would rather tell you a joke and those who would rather ask you a question. There are the glib and the tedious. So, in addition to keeping the candidate talking in a focused and meaningful way, how do you find the real person underneath it all?

It all comes under the category of *probing,* which means to search or examine, to question closely. You will always find areas you need to probe more deeply, no matter how cooperative the candidate. Remember, *you* know what you are looking for; the candidate doesn't.

When a candidate answers your question, before you move on you must ask yourself if the answer is complete. Do you need further information? Never leave a subject or area until you are fully convinced that you know everything relevant about it.

Some candidates try to tell you what they think will impress you, others simply answer questions with superficial information. Do not accept answers that fail to tell you what you need to know.

"I understand you developed a regional sales force. Tell me about that," you may ask.

"Yes, I did. It gave the company its most successful year."

The question is answered, right? No. Now you ask, "Tell me more about that. How did you develop your team? What made it the most successful year, and by what standard do you measure it?" And away you go.

By the time you finish probing for hard facts, you should know about all the people subordinate to a candidate, who did the actual work, who was truly responsible for developing the sales force, what style of management was used, whether the increased sales were truly produced by the sales force or whether there were other more basic reasons, and a lot more.

In particular, when candidates mention an accomplishment or result they have achieved, you should find out more about it, including exactly how it was achieved. Do not accept anything at face value. For instance, you may find that the increased sales resulted from the bankruptcy of the only competitor in the area.

Problem Solving

Problem solving is one of the best tools for probing. It is an attempt to present a challenging situation that the candidates might face while working for your company. The purpose is to see how they would react to or handle it. It's a method of probing the candidates' abilities, particularly their ability to think on their feet. Generally, the problem-solving questions come toward the end of the interview.

For instance, candidates for the job of production control manager might be asked, "Well, the situation is that we are working on a just-in-time manufacturing basis and we would like to improve the delivery time. How would you go about doing it? What kind of questions would you ask? What kind of information would you need?"

You are giving these applicants a problem to solve, and their reactions to your questions can tell you a lot about them as individuals. Some candidates come up with a glib solution without knowing all the facts or bothering to ask you about them. Others query you deeply about all aspects of the problem before coming up with an answer. Their reactions will obviously vary widely.

Problem solving does two things for you. First, you get a chance to see how a person thinks, and second, it sometimes happens that you may just get your problem solved.

A variation on problem solving can be used when you have candidates for some kind of manufacturing or factory position. After each interview, walk through the plant and point out some problem that is of concern to management. Then ask each candidate how he or she would go about solving it.

As you walk the floor with each candidate, you will get indications of what kind of people they are. Listen to the questions they ask. Are they bright and perceptive? If they walk through with you and don't ask any questions, you should wonder about their curiosity and involvement in that kind of operation.

Your problem-solving questions can refer to a technical problem or have something to do with management or even relationships. If you're interviewing sales candidates you could present a situation such as this: "You hear through the grapevine that a company which we are not currently doing business with is planning to double their capacity within the next six months. They've been tied in exclusively with our competitor for the past three years. Our product and prices are about the same. You know that our product would be perfect for this company. You've heard that our competitor has recently had some serious financial reversals, and you really want this order. The commission alone would be worth an additional $10,000 in your pocket. What actions would you take?''

A carefully thought-out problem such as this tests several aspects of your sales candidates' abilities. It addresses their selling skills, their integrity, and their ability to come up with workable solutions. All in all, it will tell you a lot about each person right then and there.

Problem solving is one of the most rewarding methods of probing a candidate.

Editorials

Editorials are words such as *who, what, when, where, why,* and *how.* The editorials are a form of the open-ended question, of course. They are all prompt words that solicit and probe for further information. If a candidate makes a statement such as, "Well, I really was able to build a good customer base," you can come back with, "Who were these customers, and how did you do that?"

It is simply a matter of thinking *who, what, when, where, how,* and *why* every time the candidate makes a statement. You want further explanation, you want to move toward the particulars and away from generalized statements that do not have much relevance. This technique can help you conduct an in-depth, informative interview.

How, What, Why?

Once you know a candidate's job history, the dates and places and experience, you'll have to get down to the nitty-gritty in

order to find out the person's true personal characteristics. You
need to know who the individual really is and how he or she
really performs on the job. You are, in effect, scraping away a
person's facade.

The following are samples of questions you can use to
discover more about someone's past and present. You'll notice
that none of these questions can be answered with a simple yes
or no. They all encourage the candidates to search for an
answer. Nor are the questions really direct. If you ask candidates how they will fit into your company and how they will
interact with the other people there, most of them will say,
"Fine." But if you ask them the following questions, you'll get
a more accurate, detailed picture:

1. What sort of people do you enjoy working with?
2. How do people in your work environment react to you?
3. How do your subordinates feel about you? What do
   you think they would say are your strengths and the
   areas in which you could improve?
4. Give some examples of how you get people to accomplish projects. How do you motivate them?
5. What have been the most serious problems you've had
   with *people who work for you?* How have you resolved
   them?
6. What have been the most serious problems you've had
   with *people you worked for?* How have you resolved
   them?
7. Among the people who work for you, which do you
   admire the most, and why?
8. Have you ever had to fire someone? If so, why, and
   how did you handle it?
9. Of the people working for you, how many did you hire
   yourself, and what were you looking for when you hired
   them?
10. Give five adjectives that generally describe the people
    who work for you.

A good indication of how well each candidate will perform
for you involves his attitudes toward his current position. Here
are questions to help you learn more about that:

1. What characteristics of your present job do you like? What are some of the things you don't like?
2. How would you change your job if you had the power to do so?
3. Describe the importance of your job within the company's overall business plan.
4. What reasons do you have for seeking another position?
5. Do you feel appreciated in your present job? Why do you feel that way?
6. Have you been in your current job too long? Why?
7. What are the top three accomplishments you've had in your present job? How would others view them?
8. What are the most serious problems you've had in your job, and how did you overcome them?
9. Tell me why you left each of your jobs.
10. If you had the opportunity to change anything in your work career, what would you have done differently?
11. What do you think of your current employer?
12. Name the positive factors about your present company.
13. As all companies have a personality or image, how would you describe the personality of your present company?
14. During your career, which job was the most frustrating? Why? Which job was the most rewarding or exciting? Why?
15. What bores you about your present job?
16. Do you feel you are currently being paid appropriately for your position and responsibilities?

What do the candidates really think of themselves? Here are some questions to find out:

1. Give five adjectives to describe yourself.
2. What do you consider your greatest strengths?
3. What do you consider your shortcomings, and what have you done to overcome them?
4. What motivates you to be successful?
5. How would your spouse or companion describe you relative to your work?

6. Describe where your career is heading and the direction your life has taken. Are you pleased with where you are in life right now?
7. Do you find pleasure in your work? How so?
8. Have you ever considered another career? If so, what?
9. Name something you have really wanted to do but have never been able to do, even when there was an opportunity.
10. What are your personal interests?
11. Is there anything about yourself that you are disappointed in? Why?
12. What things about yourself are you proud of?

What are each candidate's career goals? How does each individual feel about the future?

1. What responsibilities do you want, and what kind of results would you expect to achieve, in your next job?
2. What kind of responsibilities would you like to avoid in your next job?
3. Where is your whole career leading? What are your long-term goals? How do you expect to get there? Do you feel you are on the right track?

The best way to check a candidate's honesty is through references. Naturally, most candidates will not admit to dishonesty or a lack of integrity in an interview. However, here are a couple of questions that might give you some clues as to their attitudes:

1. How do you feel about exaggerating or telling a white lie to sell a product?
2. In what situations in the business environment do you feel that total honesty would be inappropriate?
3. Give some examples where you haven't been able to meet commitments, perhaps because of someone else's actions.
4. If you saw a coworker doing something dishonest, would you let your boss know about it? How would you handle it?

Facades are constructed over a long period of time, generally since a person's formative years. It is not easy to see behind them, but skillful questioning and persistence will do it.

If you look at the way these questions are worded and what they are designed to discover, you'll be able to generate similar questions of your own, ones that are tailor-made to your particular company.

The idea is to get past the image the candidate is trying to show and/or the normal social patterns the candidate uses to get along in life, in order to get as close to the truth as you can. The truth is what you are seeking, and you shouldn't be willing to settle for less.

In Chapter 13, there is an example of an interview with George Spencer, our candidate for the Western regional sales manager for the Alpha Corporation. This interview shows how to use many of the prompting and probing techniques we have discussed here.

12

It's a Wrap

You have finished the chronological part of the interview, tracking the candidate's history all the way from high school and college to the present. You've also made sure all your yellow flags have been addressed. Now, before concluding the interview, you have a number of important issues to discuss, not the least of which is compensation.

Can We Talk Money?

Interviewers are sometimes embarrassed to talk about money, but you can't afford to be shy. The best way to handle this situation is simply to ask the question; "Give me some feel for what you've been earning. What is your base salary and what is your total compensation?"

Most candidates will give you an answer, but it is your job to get even more specific. When a person says, "Yes, I'm making $95,000," you have to find out what that amount is *really* composed of. It may be $65,000 in salary, $25,000 in bonus, and $5,000 in car allowance. Some people may also throw in the value of medical and life insurance and other benefits.

Some of the candidate's compensation may be made up of stock options. If a person has been earning stock options and your company doesn't grant them, you had better know that. Indeed, some people, because of where they are in life, place a higher premium on stock options than they do on salary. Some candidates may be willing to take a lower salary in a riskier situation in order to get options. Depending on the overall financial climate, stock options may provide significant leverage, especially if the company plans to go public at some stage. Whatever the case, you should know about it.

A variety of elements can enter compensation discussions. You must find out what all your candidates have been earning and what they are looking for now. In order to negotiate effectively, you should know what is desirable and significant to each individual.

In rare instances, an applicant will refuse to talk about compensation. You may, for example, run across candidates who say, "Whatever the job pays is fine with me." Usually they say something like this for one of two reasons. On the one hand, some are being paid less than they should be for their position in life and are embarrassed by it; on the other hand, some are making a lot more and for some reason are willing to make a major sacrifice and take this job for less. Both of these situations pose yellow flags and need further investigation.

Once again, if a candidate avoids answering the compensation question in any way, you should be insistent. "Well, it's important for us to trace your accomplishments and your history and, likewise, we want to see how you've been rewarded because that adds to our understanding of where you've been in life and what your career progression has been."

The candidate may hold fast, insisting that "it's not important that you know my present compensation. It shouldn't affect this job if I am willing to accept what you pay." There's not much you can do here. You have to either accept the situation or reject the candidate. It is up to you and your assessment of all the factors that are involved in picking a winner.

When a number of people at your company interview the individual, only one person should ask about compensation. It could be someone from the human resources department or the individual to whom the candidate would report, if and when hired.

Here, again, it is important that you take notes and watch the candidates for the key factors that interest each of them. If your company is offering stock options and a candidate lights up at the idea, be sure to make a note. It will come in handy during the later negotiating stage.

Looking for the Hot Buttons

During the last part of the interview, as you're tying up many loose ends, one of your functions is to review each candidate's hot buttons. These are things about the job and the company that have excited and interested them. You have asked the candidates about their long-term goals, what things fascinate them about this job, what have been the negatives about previous positions, and other points suggested in Chapter 11.

Throughout the interview, each candidate has been giving you clues as to what has been attractive about, or what has detracted from, previous positions. These items should be noted for consideration later, when determining which candidate is best suited to your company and deciding what offer of compensation to extend.

Hot buttons differ from one candidate to another. Without attempting to analyze why one person has a particular hot button and someone else has another, here is a list of some potential hot buttons:

- Position title
- Ratio of salary to bonus
- Current cash compensation versus long-term gains
- Large office versus small office
- Reporting relationships
- Perquisites, such as car or country club membership
- Amount of travel
- Size of the particular department

Some of the candidate's positive hot buttons may be negatives to you and your company. For example, you may be a small, start-up company operating on a lean and mean budget. You maintain relatively modest salary levels, with a major portion of a person's compensation paid in stock options.

This situation would probably be unsuitable for a candidate who owned an expensive house with a large mortgage, and had two children in their first years of college. Such people need a high level of cash compensation. Their hot button is the immediate salary prospects, not the long-term payoffs.

Bringing It to a Close

After finishing the main body of the interview, your next step is to tell each candidate more about the position and the company. Allow people to ask questions at this stage, and answer them as honestly and fully as you can. Perhaps you can take selected candidates on a tour of the plant or facility. Whatever you decide to do, take note of what attracts each candidate about the job or the company. These items will help you formulate an attractive offer.

Your next step is to ask the candidates to summarize themselves by telling you in their own words where they have been and where they are going. This gives each candidate a chance to pull everything together and impress you with his or her qualifications for the job.

Several questions can prompt this summary. For example: "How would you describe your strengths, and what evidence do you have to support this?

"How would you summarize your qualifications for this position?"

This is also the time to present the viable candidates with a copy of your performance expectations, assuming that you feel there is strong interest on both sides. Ask them to review the list and comment on the entries. What more information would they need to determine if the expectations are realistic, and how would they approach meeting them? This is another form of problem solving. (Note that you might ask candidates to come back with these answers instead of having them provide you with an immediate response.)

There is one very important final question to ask. This is where you often catch something the candidate might have left out of the interview and the résumé, perhaps a short-term job held between major positions, perhaps even the lack of a college degree. Ask this final question: "Right now, I feel you're a good candidate for this position. Our personnel department does a very thorough job checking references. Do you know of any reason we could be surprised at what we find? Is there anything you haven't told us that we should know regarding your candidacy for this position?''

Asking for References

Although some candidates list one or two references on their résumés, most do not list any. Even if they have done so, you will certainly need more. Now is the time for you to ask each candidate if there are other people you can talk to. ''I'm looking for people you worked for, your peers, and people who have worked for you.''

You'll find most candidates reluctant to give you their present employer or people who work with them currently. This is understandable in most cases. But what if the candidate says, ''There is nobody I can give you. I've worked for the same company for ten years and I haven't told them I'm leaving yet.'' In response to that, you could say, ''Well, perhaps there is someone who has left the company who can serve as a reference.'' If you pursue this line of questioning, you will ultimately be given the names of some people you can talk to.

If difficulties continue, however, say, ''We're very interested in you as a candidate, but we are going to have to talk to some people about you to verify all this information and to get their opinions. What can we do about it?'' Generally, the candidate will come up with some kind of references.

Reference checking is a skill in itself; it will be detailed in Chapter 15.

This brings you to the close of the interview, at which point you either turn the candidates over to someone else for a further interview or send them on their way. If you feel truly interested in a candidate, it is wise at this point to say so, perhaps even scheduling another interview so that you can talk once again.

Be encouraging to the top candidates. Tell them that there are several people you are looking at but that they are probably within the top four or five. Generally, of course, you would not be in a position to say that to the first person you see. In such cases, you could say, "Look, we like you, but you're the first person we've seen and it may be two or three weeks before we see the rest of the candidates. We'll keep you posted as to where we are. Feel free to call me, and I'll be happy to give you an update."

Final Impressions

It is important to you that all the candidates leave your office with a very positive impression of both you and the company. Keep in mind that each candidate, even if not hired, could be a source for other candidates, could refer customers to your company, or could even become a customer or affect your customers in some way.

It is far more desirable that people speak positively about your company rather than negatively. A candidate who leaves with negative impressions may come back to haunt you. What you want is to have candidates who end up saying, "That is the best company I ever got turned down by."

The way to have candidates leave with positive impressions is to treat them with respect, to meet them on time, to treat them the way you would want to be treated, and to follow all those other common patterns of social behavior that come under the general heading of good manners. Make all the candidates feel that the company did a good job presenting itself and that it looked like the kind of place they would have enjoyed working for.

13

A Likely Candidate for Alpha

George W. Spencer is a candidate for the position of Western regional sales manager for Alpha Corporation. Here is an abbreviated version of the interview that might be conducted with him. Consult both the Alpha Profile (Chapter 4) and Spencer's résumé (Chapter 8) as you read this.

The interviewer, the Alpha vice-president of sales, meets Mr. Spencer in the lobby and ushers him into his private office. The following is a synopsis of the interview he conducts:

INTERVIEW WITH GEORGE W. SPENCER
Candidate for the Position of Western
Regional Sales Manager
Alpha Corporation

Vice-President:	Did you have any trouble finding our offices? The numbering system on these buildings is a little confusing.
Spencer:	No, your directions were perfect. In fact, I used to have a customer in this complex.
VP:	Oh, who was that?

S: Super Drugs. They have their divisional offices in the building. We did some training with their local controller.

VP: I've seen the company, but I haven't met any of their people. Would you like some coffee or a soft drink?

S: No, thanks.

VP: George, do you mind if I take some notes during the interview?

S: No, that's fine.

VP: What I would like us to accomplish during the next hour or so is to determine if we have something that would be of interest to both of us. You know we are looking for a regional sales manager. I'd like to find out as much as I can about your background, experience, and interests. And then I'll tell you about the position and Alpha. At the conclusion of our meeting, we can then determine if further discussions would be beneficial to both you and our company.

To begin with, why don't you tell me about your education. I'd like to know how you did in school, your involvement in outside activities, and any other items you felt were significant during your school years. Then we'll continue on with your work experience.

S: Where would you like me to start?

VP: Start with high school and proceed on through college.

S: High school was okay. My grades were average. I worked part-time and lettered in two sports, tennis and track. In fact, I was offered a partial scholarship in tennis at the University of Wisconsin.

VP: What prompted your decision to go to college?

S: I guess it was just a natural thing to go on to college. Most all the students in our high school went on to college.

VP: Most all the students went on to college?

S: Yes. We grew up in a middle-class neighborhood, and I guess most of the parents, like mine, had always talked like college was just an extension of our learning. Nothing special; we just were going to go on. I never gave it a second thought.

VP: What kind of work did you do while you were going to high school?

S: I had the usual paper route for about two years, then got a job at a local drugstore. Most of the time I stocked shelves, but later I spent more time assisting customers in their purchases. This wasn't a big chain store, just a small, independent business. Mr. Yeager, the owner, kind of took me under his wing and showed me some of the ropes of the business.

VP: Showed you some of the ropes of the business?

S: Yes. He even had me do some reordering with the salesmen. Maybe that was the first time I got some feel for what salesmen do for a living.

VP: After you were graduated from high school, what curriculum or field did you think you would pursue in college?

S: My father is an engineering manager for a chemical company. He wanted me to go into engineering. But my interests, and consequently my grades, were not the best in the sciences or math. They were all right, but I didn't really enjoy these classes. I just wanted to get into college and see what it was all about.

VP: How did you like college? Was it what you expected? How did you finally select business as a major?

S: I had fun the first two years in college. Joined a fraternity. Played tennis. And even found time to study. I started in a liberal arts program, and then an economics course got me interested in business. By my junior year I had switched to the business school. Accounting was a lot different from calculus and algebra. I liked it, and it came easy. Marketing courses reminded me of my work at the drugstore. I got serious about business and pursued my degree in business.

VP: What kind of grades did you receive?

S: I had a 3.0 in my major, with an overall grade point of 2.8.

VP: What did you do after you received your degree?

S: I accepted a position with Zeron in Chicago.

VP: Why Zeron? Did you have any other offers?

S: I took the usual interviews on the campus, looking for a sales or marketing position. At the time of my decision, I had three offers. Zeron represented an unusual opportunity for me.

VP: An unusual opportunity?

S: As you know, Zeron is a national company, selling sophisticated audio-visual equipment to high schools and colleges throughout the country. The opportunity described to me was to get right in the trenches and sell equipment. Of course, this was after a six-week training program. What I liked about it was that within a short period of time I would either prove my sales ability or think about another career.

VP: It sounds like you laid it all on the line with Zeron, George.

S: Perhaps I did. The recruiter on campus, as well as the people I had met in the company during my interviews, were young, dynamic, aggressive—I guess my image of what a salesman should be, or what I envisioned as my image.

VP: Tell me about your progression with Zeron, specifically giving some examples of your accomplishments.

S: I spent all three years in Chicago. That was after completing the training program at the Minneapolis headquarters. I started selling to high schools in the Greater Chicago area. Although my initial territory was certainly not a new one, I was quite successful in introducing some new equipment. As a matter of fact, I received the "Rookie of the Year" Award for my first full year of sales in 1978.

VP: Why do you think you were so successful?

S: I think . . . no, I know that I am very motivated to be on top. Pride, and certainly money, keep me anxious to be better than the next person. I typically put in long hours, often making my first sales call before eight A.M. I seldom finished before six in the evening.

VP: Putting in hours, alone, doesn't necessarily make it happen. What techniques did you use to close sales?

S: First, I educated myself about the buying habits of that particular school and other schools in that district. I found out the budget parameters for a/v equipment. When I walked in to make a presentation, I had all the facts.

Second, I made sure that I had established good rapport with the buying personnel. I got to know them through various school associations.

And third, I knew my product.

Note: To shorten this interview example, we will move on in time to continue the interview with George completing a discussion about his current position. The vice-president of sales has covered each position and has found out when he worked at each, at least in terms of months of employment. The interviewer has not accepted at face value the dates given on the résumé, to ensure there are no gaps. He has also been noting success patterns and personal characteristics, both on the job as well as in education. These will later be compared to the Profile.

VP: George, why are you interested in leaving Financial Management Systems?

S: I'm not sure that I want to leave. Your ad in *The Wall Street Journal* sounded interesting.

VP: What specifically interested you?

S: Alpha appears to be a young, fast-growing company. The position of Western regional manager should encompass a broader scope than my current position. It's more of a ground-floor opportunity.

VP:	Why do you think you may be qualified for the position? What are your strengths? What would you bring to Alpha?
S:	You sell to colleges and universities. I'm familiar with selling to educational institutions. I also have had considerable experience selling computer systems with Financial Management Systems. I feel confident that I can make a strong contribution to your sales organization.
VP:	George, you now have several people working for you, salespeople and a support team. The position we have at Alpha has minimal supervisory responsibility. How do you feel about that?
S:	Alpha seems to be a fast-growing company. I would suspect that within a short period of time you will need more direct sales people. My experience in hiring and training new people would pay off. I'm good at selecting top sales types. Perhaps it is a sixth sense, but I have had excellent success in building a strong sales team.
VP:	Are you ready to go back to direct selling yourself?
S:	Sure. This is the kind of opportunity that I've been looking for.
VP:	What kind of opportunity is that?
S:	Getting in on the ground floor. Being a big fish in a little pond. I have done it all before for large companies. Now I can put it to work for a smaller company where I can make a difference in the early success.
VP:	What do you believe to be the major differences between working in a large company and a firm the size of Alpha?

S: I imagine you need to operate on a lean and mean basis. You need to watch the expenses and make every dollar count. You need to put in long hours, which I always have in the past. You have fewer people to rely on for support, and thus you need to operate at all levels . . . from sweeping the floor to dealing with top executives within customer organizations. In short, you do everything that is necessary to make it happen.

VP: How would you summarize your career up to this point in time? And what do you see for yourself in the future?

Note: George summarizes his sales and management career, again emphasizing his interest in joining a young, growing company like Alpha.

VP: George, you seem to have all the right answers. It is very important for us to hire the right person for this position. I would like to talk to some references before we continue our discussions. Would you provide me with the names of people to whom you reported, some peers, and a few people that you hired and who worked for you?

S: I'm sure that I can give you a list of people to contact. However, I want to keep this inquiry confidential, and therefore it would be difficult to give you names at my present employer.

VP: Are there people who have left Financial Management Systems within the past year or two who know you?

S: Yes, there are a few. I'll find out where they are and give you their names.

| VP: | If I were to talk to your current bosses at some later date when we are further down the line, what do you think they would say about your performance? |

Note: George then discusses what several people at his company might say about him.

| VP: | George, the one thing that would concern me would be any information I might obtain from these references that does not concur with what you have said thus far. Will I find any surprises? |
| S: | I don't think so. |

Note: The vice-president of sales then tells George all about Alpha, its growth plans, and the Western territory.

VP:	I would like to give you a list of the performance expectations that we have developed for this position. Review these items, and at our next meeting you can tell me how you might approach achieving these expectations and what you would expect from Alpha to make them happen.
S:	I'll be traveling next week, but I'll call you to set up another meeting. Could you give me some literature on Alpha's products and any other information that I can study?
VP:	Yes. My secretary has a package of information which includes product literature, company information, and a description of our benefits program. One more thing before you leave: Would you tell me about your current compensation package?
S:	Last year I earned approximately $85,000.
VP:	How much of that was salary and how much was bonus?

S: My base salary is $65,000, the rest was bonus. I also receive a car allowance of $450 per month.

VP: George, I believe we have had a very profitable first meeting. When you return, I would like you to meet several of the other executives here at Alpha. We are seeing several candidates, such as yourself, and hope to complete our selection process by the end of next month. Do you have any other questions?

S: No. You have filled me in quite well. I look forward to our next meeting.

14

Closing the Loop

One problem people face when they gather information is how to evaluate it. How do you differentiate between what's important and what isn't? What do you measure it against? How do you distinguish between fact and opinion? How do you judge the accuracy of the information you have? And how do you apply the information to the task at hand?

The PIE System takes these common difficulties into account by simplifying them and making them easily confrontable in the third and final phase: Evaluate.

You have found your candidates, interviewed them all, and decided who will be disqualified and who will be among the finalists still worthy of consideration. Only the prime candidates are left. It's time to evaluate them more closely.

The Envelope, Please

The first step in the third phase of the PIE Selection System is to compare the final candidates against the Profile and then against each other. The primary tool used to make this comparison is the Candidate Evaluation Form (see Figure 3) which was filled in by each interviewer shortly after meeting with each candidate.

The evaluation form has three purposes:

1. To rate the candidate's success patterns and personal characteristics against the Profile

Figure 3. Candidate Evaluation Form.

ALPHA CORPORATION
CANDIDATE EVALUATION FORM

REGIONAL SALES MANAGER

CANDIDATE NAME _____ DATE _____

INSTRUCTIONS: For each of the SUCCESS PATTERNS and PERSONAL
CHARACTERISTICS, indicate to what extent, if any, the candidate meets
the stated requirements.

> COMPLETELY —No question in your mind
> MODERATELY—Most likely, but not certain on all
>   aspects
> DOUBTFUL —Does not have

> Leave BLANK if you did not find out.

> Refer to the complete PROFILE for full definitions.

	Completely	Moderately	Doubtful
SUCCESS PATTERNS			
1. $2 million/yr sales record*	____	____	____
2. Computer systems to end-users	____	____	____
3. Sales to universities*	____	____	____
4. Developed new accounts*	____	____	____
5. Completed college degree*	____	____	____
6. Customer relations	____	____	____
PERSONAL CHARACTERISTICS			
1. Integrity and honesty*	____	____	____
2. High energy level	____	____	____
3. Verbal communication skills/ presence*	____	____	____
4. Drive/determination to win*	____	____	____
5. Customer orientation	____	____	____
6. "Chemistry" with team*	____	____	____
7. Well-organized	____	____	____
8. Self-starter*	____	____	____

*Absolutes.

(continues)

Figure 3. (Continued.)

COMMENTS _____

_____

SUMMARY STATEMENT _____

_____

YOUR CHOICE: Thumbs up? _____ Thumbs down? _____ Or? _____

Signed by
Interviewer _____

    2. To match the evaluation of one candidate against that of another or others

    3. To compare the evaluations of several people who have interviewed the same candidate

The Candidate Evaluation Form provides an easy method of scoring the candidates in all pertinent areas. Each interviewer should independently fill out this form for each candidate as soon as possible after the interview. Everyone's immediate impressions should be recorded while still fresh, especially if an interviewer sees more than one candidate on the same day. When all interviews have been completed, all the forms are collected by the person in charge of the hiring project, who compares and reconciles the different evaluations.

Under the success patterns and personal characteristics are listed all criteria that have been developed in the Profile. The example in Figure 3 contains lists from the Alpha Profile completed in an earlier chapter. (These have been abbreviated to fit onto the form.) In addition to listing the success patterns and personal characteristics from the Profile, you need to mark with an asterisk those attributes that are the absolutes. The remainder are, of course, pluses.

Taking each success pattern and personal characteristic in turn as you fill in the form, analyze what you learned during the interview process and indicate whether the candidate has that pattern or characteristic—completely, moderately, or doubtful.

If you are certain the candidate has the required attribute, put a check in the Completely column. Check the Moderately column if you think the person has some of the attribute. And if you think the candidate has little or no trace of the attribute, check the Doubtful column. If you didn't find out, leave the columns blank.

The third column, Doubtful, means that during the course of the interview you uncovered the fact that the candidate does not have the personal characteristic or success pattern under consideration. Also check the Doubtful column if it is very unlikely, from your conversation with the candidate, that he or she has this particular attribute. An obvious example is when a success pattern calls for a person to have "Completed a degree in a technical field" and the candidate has not graduated from college.

A less obvious example might be found under personal characteristics. If the need is for "good verbal and written communications skills" and the candidate's presentation in the interview was poor—perhaps because of nervousness—and if you have not seen much evidence of the candidate's written words, then you would check Doubtful against this attribute.

Below this assessment section is a space for comments. You may want to note a desire to see the candidate again, or you might express doubts: "I don't feel good about him in spite of the success patterns." This is a catchall section where, for instance, you can list your concerns, pointing out areas where you felt there were not enough data.

The summary statement section allows the interviewer to sum up the candidate. This section could include such comments as "This is the most viable candidate, the one with all of the success patterns and most of the personal characteristics," or vice versa. It is generally a one-sentence statement about the candidate.

The final section, Your Choice, allows you to make a decision. It is self-evident that thumbs up means you want to pursue the candidate further, thumbs down means that you are no longer interested in this person. The "or" category could mean that you feel the need for further investigation of one or more areas.

The evaluation is as simple as that—if you have done all the steps correctly. Now you have a completed evaluation of each candidate. The beauty of the PIE System is that once you know exactly what you are looking for, it's not all that hard to recognize it when you see it or, on the other hand, to know when you do not have it.

Some people like to use a numerical system for rating or weighing candidates. This is not recommended because it can be misleading. If you measured each asset in numbers and then added up the columns, you might find one candidate with 324 points and another with 320. But is the "winning" candidate really better than the "loser"? You could end up making the wrong choice.

For one thing, the candidate who scored 320 may have rated higher than the other on certain key factors. Even though they may have only been pluses, not absolutes, they may have been more important than the pluses on which the other candidate rated higher. On the other hand, if you like the idea of points and are clever enough to set up an accurate system, it may work for you.

In the PIE System, the absolutes and the pluses are important. Theoretically, any candidate who does not have all the absolutes should be removed from consideration. But sometimes no candidate can be found with all the absolutes. Consequently, we may decide to change one absolute to a plus, thus being more realistic in our recruitment effort.

Suppose you find two candidates A and B, with all the absolutes but only five of six desired pluses. If candidate A's pluses are all significant ones and candidate B has one plus that is less significant, we may well pick A for the job.

It is important to remember that during this final step you are judging the candidates based upon what you discovered during the interview. For the purposes of evaluation, at this point *you assume that the information is accurate.* If it isn't, everything changes. (Your impressions may be altered by what other interviewers have discovered or by what you find out when checking references.)

This second, most vital phase of the Evaluation process involves the checking of references. As you will see in the next chapter, there is much more involved than simply confirming the title and time in which the candidate held a particular job. It requires a far more thoroughgoing procedure. No final judgment can be made about the candidate until this step has been completed.

To restate the Evaluation process simply, first you compare the candidate to the Profile, then you compare the evaluation forms completed by all who interviewed the candidate in the company, and finally you compare the candidates one against the other.

Comparing different views of the same candidate can be difficult. Because of different approaches, the results can be wildly dissimilar between one interviewer and the next. This is usually resolved by communication afterward among all the interviewers.

Perceptions may differ, and interviewing skills certainly will. One interviewer may have established a better rapport with the candidate and discovered more information. Another might have delved into something in the candidate's past that the others overlooked. If the interviewers sit down and talk about the candidate, all this will become known. In the final analysis, agreement has to be reached by consensus. When all the facts are known to all the interviewers, this should not be difficult.

In the final step, comparing the two top candidates, we take the composite picture given by all the evaluations of one candidate and compare it to the composite evaluations of the other candidate. It is like laying one grid on top of another. We then judge where one candidate is stronger than the other, or if they have similar strengths. Except in the highly unusual circumstance of a dead heat, by this point one candidate should be preferred over the other.

The success patterns and personal characteristics you are comparing have been developed from the performance expectations or the objectives of the job, the results you want to achieve. Thus, it wouldn't hurt to refer to those performance expectations again, with the intention of judging if the person can really meet them. No step in the PIE System is independent of the other steps. You always compare back and forth, with the Profile being the foundation of it all.

It is during the final phase of judgment that an important, somewhat intangible factor enters the picture. It is sometimes called "gut feel," "sixth sense," or "strong hunch," but it is more accurately called "intuition."

Intuition

Intuition is defined in some dictionaries as "direct perception of truth, fact, etc., independent of any reasoning process." It comes from a Latin root word meaning "contemplation."

Intuition is direct perception or quick insight. It has very little to do with logic, on the face of it. Those who are in love with logic tend to ignore it, but it is a dangerous gift to shun. In the selection process, intuition works both ways: You can have either a positive or a negative feeling about a candidate.

At times, something may bother you about a candidate, something you can't explain. This something, whatever it is, cannot be ignored. Discuss it with the other interviewers and see if anyone else sensed it. Chances are that at least two out of three, for instance, will have sensed something. And perhaps the other person will be better able to define the problem or concern.

You must listen to intuition. It plays an important part in the hiring process. Even when you have done all the right things throughout the process, if that niggling voice whispers in your ear, you must check it out. If you cannot clear it up in your mind when you are making your choice of candidates, if you have reexamined everything and you still cannot spot the source of your feeling, and if the doubts persist, you are better off not hiring the person.

Intuition is often based upon fact and experience on a subconscious level. It isn't just something that appears out of the blue, even though you may not know its source. Intuition about candidates may come from what you have seen in past candidates or workers or even from something you observed or heard during the interview that you are not quite aware of.

But you must be able to separate intuition and prejudice. Although you may not be aware of it, a candidate may look like or remind you of a former boss or colleague you didn't get along with very well. Try not to let past personal problems interfere with good judgment in the present.

Intuition is a powerful force in business. Many executives constantly use it to make decisions. Show me an executive who waits for all the facts and I'll show you an executive who has trouble making decisions. True, everyone needs facts in order to make a wise decision, but some intuition is always involved. And the selection of employees is no different from any other area of business.

Don't ignore your intuition. It's important.

15

Illusion or Reality?

One of the activities our litigious society has thrown a pall over is the checking of references. Such checking today demands a great many skills, not the least of which is circumventing this fear of litigation. The fact is that many employers are afraid to criticize former employees for fear of being sued.

There are a number of different ways to handle this formidable barrier. If you ask the candidate for permission to talk to a former employer, you can also ask for a written release granting this permission. The form might specify that the candidate agrees not to hold the person who gives the reference liable for anything he or she might say. Whether or not this would hold up in court depends on circumstances, but at least it should reassure the former company.

According to a June 1989 article in *Inc.*,* "Prospective employers check references on only 25 percent of job candidates, citing that they don't expect the former employer to cooperate as their number-one reason for not bothering to check."

The same article points out, however, that defamation, which many of these suits are based upon, is "saying, writing, or otherwise communicating any untrue or derogatory statement that may harm a person's reputation." The key word there is "untrue." Truth is a complete and absolute defense to any

* Marisa Manley, "Information Please: How to Give Useful Job References Without Getting Into Hot Water."

defamation claim. Anyone who gives specific factual statements about the candidate's former job performance is protected.

It may be difficult to get even positive information. Some companies have a blanket policy of not giving out any judgment, perhaps because of a bad experience in the past. Sometimes they are reluctant to open up because they don't really know who is calling. It could even be the candidate or his attorney! Even in cases where personnel departments are willing to share the information in the candidate's file, it is often all secondhand data and of limited value.

You need to find ways to get around these barriers. You cannot make good decisions without basic data on a candidate's track record.

Is What You See What You Get?

If reference checking is a lot of trouble, as some companies believe it is, be assured that it is worth the effort. Skillful checking of references now can save you big trouble down the line. The hiring supervisor and/or the PIE "leader" (which may be the human resources department) should be the ones to check references. It is vital. It must be done.

Reference checking is simply another form of interviewing. Once you learn how to conduct an interview by using the tools in the PIE System, you will also know how to get information from people recommended as references by candidates. Your questions may be more pointed and direct than in the interview process, but you still follow the basic system, following such rules as avoiding questions that can be answered with a yes or no. There will, of course, be exceptions to the rules. A good question to ask is "Would you rehire this person?" followed by a why or why not? Of course, you will use all your other tools to probe and to prompt.

Just as in interviewing, the key to reference checking is listening properly. Sometimes people are unwilling to make an overt negative statement about a candidate, but they will hint at it.. If you are listening properly, you'll pick up the hint and then follow through as far as possible. You must also remember that people have personal likes and dislikes, so it's important to be able to distinguish between opinion and fact.

In some cases, when you're checking references, you will find extremely cooperative people on the other end of the telephone line. In fact, you'll find that the candidate has already talked to the references and alerted them to expect your call. The positive aspect of this is that the people are receptive to your call, but the negative is that the candidate might even have told them what to say. You have to ask the right questions. A statement from the reference that the candidate is "a good guy" is not enough. You have to delve and dig and probe.

Here, as a base to build on, is a list of ten questions you should always ask each reference about every candidate:

1. How and when did you know the candidate, and what was your relationship?

2. Trace the candidate's progress/relationship with you/ your company.

3. What were the candidate's most significant accomplishments? (You want individual results, not departmental accomplishments.)

4. What were the major strengths you noted in the candidate?

5. We all have some shortcomings or areas that can be improved upon. What were the candidate's shortcomings, and how did s/he accommodate them?

6. Why did the candidate leave your company? (Or why might s/he be thinking of leaving?)

7. How would you describe the candidate's relationships with others? (This includes peers, subordinates, customers, and any others who might be appropriate.)

8. We are considering the candidate for a position that involves —— (describe the performance expectations). From your experience working with the candidate, how do you feel s/he would contribute to and meet these performance expectations? And why?

9. In summary, how would you describe the candidate's employment with your company and where would you rank the candidate in comparison with others in similar positions? Would you want to work for or with this person again? In what kind of environment?

10. Who else in your company should we talk to about the candidate?

One of the most important questions is the tenth. You need to get beyond the first tier of names given to you by the candidate. Once you start digging, you'll find there is less likely to be bias, pro or con. You could even ask for the names of people outside the company to contact, such as clients or customers who know the candidate well.

Don't overlook customers, particularly in any job involving sales. Not only are they one of your most productive sources for reference data, but they are also usually more willing to discuss the candidate than are those within the company.

When you hit a yellow or red flag, keep a note and then pursue it with the other people you talk to.

It is all much like networking. One person will often lead you to someone else. It is even easier if the candidate is high on the executive level, for such people will have reputations. Co-workers, customers, competitors—any number of people will know at least something about such people.

George W. Spencer's References

Let's return to our Alpha Corporation candidate George Spencer. He has been back to Alpha for interviews with others, including the president, and Alpha has interviewed seven other candidates. At this point, George and one other person are in final contention for the position. References will play an important factor in making the final choice. The vice president of sales for Alpha is making the inquiries.

Reference Conversation With Victoria Corley, Vice-President of Sales and Former Regional Sales Manager for Zeron Corporation

After introducing himself and telling Mrs. Corley the nature of the phone call, the Alpha vice-president begins the reference inquiry.

VP: How long have you known George, and what was your relationship to him?

Corley: I believe that George worked for us toward the end of the seventies. I remember him well, but the exact dates would need to be checked.

VP: I would appreciate it if we could confirm his employment dates at the end of our phone conversation.

C: Yes, that would be fine. I'll transfer you to our personnel department when we're through. But to get back to your question, George reported directly to me when I was the regional sales manager.

VP: Did he report to you during his entire employment with Zeron?

C: Yes, except for the three months in training here in Minneapolis.

VP: I know it's been over ten years ago, but perhaps you could tell me how George progressed during his tenure with Zeron.

C: George was a fast learner. I would call him a born salesman. He had the charisma and aggressiveness to get in to see anyone he wanted to meet. And he did his homework beforehand.

VP: His homework beforehand?

C: Yes. He made sure that he had our complete history about the school—what equipment they had; what had transpired on previous sales calls; and what was budgeted for new equipment purchases by the school board. What we didn't have, he would find on his own. He was well prepared.

VP: What results did all this preparation achieve for George?

C: He made "Rookie of the Year" his first year. Not bad when you consider we had over 50 salespeople at that time. But, besides the award, it gave him tremendous self-confidence. He went on the next two years with as great success, and he was always one of the top three salespeople in the country. For someone his age, George made a lot of money.

VP: How much did he earn?

C: Between his base salary and bonus, he must have earned at least $45,000. That was pretty good back in the seventies.

VP: You've hit on some of his strengths, but what do you feel were his shortcomings back then?

C: You know, in training we try to teach people how to become effective salespeople, and then we saddle them with a lot of paperwork. I'm from the old school. Let your top people concentrate on selling, and provide some clerk to do the paperwork. Now, of course, it's all done by computers. George could really sell. But he hated the paperwork—call reports and that sort of thing. He knew the details he had to have before each call, but he was terrible on completing the details on call reports. If there was one thing that I had to work with him on, it was making sure he left a paper trail for the next action.

VP: Was this a problem?

C: Not really—just something he had to work on.
           I would guess that with success and maturity
           he now understands the importance of this
           aspect of selling.

VP: Why did George leave Zeron?

C: George was doing very well as a salesman.
           There was another salesman that was running
           neck and neck with George in terms of sales.
           When we needed to promote someone to my
           position as the regional sales manager in Chi-
           cago, I selected the other person. He was a
           couple of years senior to George in experience
           and had an edge of maturity. I think that
           George was very disappointed. Remember, he
           is a very competitive person. He did not want
           to work for the promoted salesperson. They
           were peers, and it was difficult for George to
           make that shift in roles. I tried to keep him.
           Even offered him a territory in another region.
           But he decided to leave.

VP: How did George get along with others in the
           company and with customers?

C: George seemed to get along with everyone.
           Even the salesperson who was promoted was
           sorry to see George leave. Customers enjoyed
           working with him. In fact, we lost one major
           account after George left. I found out later that
           we might have kept that account if George
           had still been with us.

VP: We are interviewing George for a regional
           sales manager position. *[The Alpha vice-
           president then reviews the performance ex-
           pectations from the Profile].* Would you com-
           ment on how you think George could handle
           this position?

C: I would think that George is certainly capable
           of meeting your expectations. I would guess

that he has matured by this time to the point that he has probably managed people and has some sort of track record there. I can't vouch for that from his experience with us. But I would be very surprised if he hasn't done extremely well in his career.

VP: How would you summarize your views on George, and would you hire him again?

C: George was quite a talented salesperson. I've even used him as a model when interviewing other salespeople. I don't know how good a manager he is, but I sure would want to take a look at him if an appropriate position became available in our company. Where did you say he was working now?

VP: What would you consider would be an appropriate position for him?

C: As I said, I would assume he has been a sales manager. I would certainly talk to him regarding some sales management position.

VP: I'll tell George you asked about him. Is there anyone else I should speak to about George's performance at Zeron?

C: Yes. That regional sales manager we promoted over George is now president of a company out in your area. He always regretted that George left. You might want to contact him. And one customer still asks about George. I'll get her phone number for you.

Mrs. Corley provides the phone numbers and then, after the Alpha man thanks her for her time and candid remarks, transfers the call to the personnel records department for verification of George's dates of employment.

Before the Alpha vice-president proceeded to contact the two names given him by Mrs. Corley, as well as other

references on George, he summarized the reference information.

1. George appears to be a topnotch salesperson.
2. Customers and other employees of Zeron liked him.
3. George was very aggressive and ambitious.
4. He knew how to prepare for the sales call.
5. He didn't like paperwork. (What salesperson does?)

The Alpha vice-president also wanted to list some specific questions he would present to the other, more recent employment references. We are not just considering George for a sales position, he thought, but for a managerial position.

1. What is his managerial style?
2. Is he a team player?
3. Has he actually accomplished what he said he has?
4. Can he control sales costs?
5. Can he maintain profit margins?
6. Why is he really considering leaving his present position?
7. What do recent customers think of him?
8. Has he plateaued in his career, or can he continue to grow?
9. What will challenge him at Alpha?
10. What will it take to get him?

George had given Alpha one or two names at each company where he had worked. The vice-president thought that, depending on what he found, he would try to talk with at least eight or nine references, several of whom had not been referred by George himself.

George's current employment references would be handled through contact with two people, a sales manager and a customer service person, both of which had left within the past three months to join a competitor. The vice-president felt that these two people would lead him to others. George had also noted the names of two of his present customers. His relationship with them would result in their treating the inquiry confidential.

If no red flags appeared, Alpha would be able to make a decision within a week.

There's Always One More

There are many references to be checked. If people you talk to keep on giving you the names of more people, the process could go on for a long, long time. When should you be satisfied? Is there a magic number when you stop?

The magic number doesn't exist. The point to stop is when you are completely satisfied that you know who each candidate is, that they are or are not as they have presented themselves, and that you feel that they can (or cannot) do the job.

In checking out a candidate for vice-president of sales, one company found that he had an excellent sales record and looked like a good winner. The president had talked to three or four topnotch references, including personal friends that dated back ten years, and they were all laudatory. But intuition warned him to keep going. He had a funny feeling about the candidate. It wasn't based on anything concrete, but it was too strong to ignore. He kept on checking.

It must have been the fifth or sixth reference he had talked to. Suddenly, out of the blue, the person said, "I don't trust that guy." In a way it surprised the president, but considering his intuitive feeling, it shouldn't have.

The reference was a customer of the candidate. After further prodding, the reference said, "You'd better check out this guy's expenses." More prodding. The customer finally said he thought this man was dishonest in his reimbursable expenses. More probing. "Well, I know he put me on an expense account as going to Hawaii with him when in fact I never went."

The confession unleashed him. He added. "You should also check a certain buyer in this electronics firm who—Just check with her."

The president thanked the customer, got the buyer's telephone number, and called her. She didn't hesitate to say that she considered the salesman a pest and never wanted to see him again.

By pursuing references, the president learned some interesting facts. On the positive side, this man had an enviable sales record. But the president valued integrity and had high moral standards, so he was not interested in someone who cheated on the company he worked for and "messed around" with women buyers to the point of harassment.

Another example underscores the point that part of your reference checking should include the examination of academic references. If a person claims to have a degree, you must verify it.

A company in the scientific area needed a financial executive. The other executives in the company were all highly educated—most had master's degrees or Ph.D.s. One candidate uncovered by the human resources manager seemed to be an ideal candidate in many ways. But the manager had trouble verifying her B.A. degree with the college she named in her résumé. When he called her, she insisted she had the degree and that the college must be making a mistake. He and his staff probably spent a good three hours trying to verify that degree, but in the end, they couldn't confirm it.

He called her again and told her that he couldn't verify the degree. "Until we can do so, we can't consider you a candidate," he said.

Two days later, she called the HR manager and said, "I've got to confess, I don't have a degree."

"Why did you lie about it?" he asked, both frustrated and bemused.

"Well, you impressed upon me that all the people in the company were highly educated, and I thought they wouldn't be interested in me if I didn't have a university education."

It was ironic. The human resources manager had been so impressed with the candidate that he had recommended her to his management. They had been very interested in her background, and they would have been just as interested without the degree.

He had to drop her as a candidate because she had lied. She lost a very attractive position that she probably would have attained. All her other references were impeccable, and her track record was outstanding. It was a shame, but the company just felt they couldn't trust her, particularly in a financially responsible position.

Exaggeration of past accomplishments is another problem that can be uncovered as you check references. In particular, professional résumé writers often do a disservice to their clients by portraying them as being able to handle higher-level jobs than they are qualified for. Admittedly, résumés are a marketing tool. It's fine to put a candidate's record in the best possible light, but the facts should not be distorted.

Most people do not tell outright lies on their résumés, but they sometimes do stretch the facts or present only a partial picture. It's important that you uncover any such maneuvers, regardless of whether they were intended or inadvertent.

In checking references, one recruiter talked to someone at a candidate's previous place of employment. When she asked whether they had checked the candidate's references before he was hired, the reference replied, "Oh, yes, I called the So-and-So Company, and they confirmed what he said."

This puzzled the recruiter because the candidate had not told her that he had worked for the "So-and-So Company." In fact, she had uncovered a short-term position in the candidate's background that he had chosen to omit from his record.

When she went back to the candidate and asked him about it, he said, "Oh, I just didn't think that was important, so I didn't mention it." This is usually the excuse when something is missing.

Money Talk

The toughest thing to confirm during a reference check is information about compensation. Probably the only way you are going to get such verification is to ask candidates to bring in their W-2 form from the previous year. As a practical matter, however, most employers do not have the nerve to do that.

Most companies will not give you a compensation figure. Personnel departments have accurate records, but they won't reveal compensation information. They sometimes will confirm a figure the candidate gave you. The typical manager often doesn't remember, because you're not usually talking about a current employee.

Generally, compensation information is considered private. The best way to confirm compensation is to say casually, "He indicated that he was earning about $70,000 working for you. Is this in the ballpark?" The person you are talking to will probably say, "That sounds about right." Occasionally, of course, someone will say, "He's really stretching that one."

You can often get an answer more easily this way than to ask bluntly what the candidate was earning.

Remember the key phrase in checking references—just one more. Don't stop calling people until you are absolutely certain that you have discovered everything that it is possible and proper for you to discover about the candidate.

By the time you finish this step, you will have almost completed the process of the PIE System. It's an exciting time. The reward for all your work is in view. The field of candidates has narrowed down to two or three people who have met your criteria in terms of personal characteristics and success patterns. They have all the absolutes and should be able to meet your performance expectations.

You are now in a position to make a selection from a group of winners.

16

After the Right Choice

The following tale of woe could be titled:

How *Not* to Sell Your Company to a Candidate

Frank was being recruited as director of engineering for a major company within his industry. His present employer was over 2,000 miles away, but Frank was willing to relocate. Frank was known by the many vendors who called on him, some of whom covered the whole United States.

This was the setting for how not to sell a candidate. The scenario that follows was described to me by Frank.

As instructed, Frank arrived at the company's facility early in the morning. Upon arrival, he was asked to sign in the log book at the receptionist desk, where all visitors sign in. During the ten to fifteen minutes he waited in the lobby, Frank ran into a vendor who had recently called on him at his current place of employment. Frank was embarrassed to see her because he had not told any of his associates that he was considering a job change.

During the day, Frank met with company executives. Several times he was left outside an executive's office, waiting for the next interviewer to meet with him.

Throughout the entire day, no one had discussed the position for which he was being interviewed, even though the company had developed a Profile that included specific performance expectations. The position was to replace an existing executive who was moving on to another assignment.

Toward the end of the day, Frank met with the human resources manager and asked her to define the position. She began to describe a position subordinate to the one for which Frank thought he was being considered. At that point, controlling his fury, Frank asked to speak to the vice-president with whom he had met earlier in the day.

In some very clear terms he told the vice-president how they had wasted his time and that he had no interest in being considered for a position with a company that didn't know what it was looking for.

When the president of the company heard of how Frank's day had been mishandled, he, too, was angry. The company had made a terrible impression on this important candidate. Subsequently, he made changes in the procedures for the treatment of professional applicants. Perhaps some of these changes, as enumerated below, would apply to your company.

Now Let's Do It Right

First, each candidate should be assigned a specific coordinator responsible for the candidate the entire time he/she is there. This would include meeting the candidate upon arrival; obtaining a badge; registering the candidate in a special, confidential log book not available to anyone walking into the lobby; and acquainting the candidate with the schedule for the day. This coordinator could either be the hiring executive or someone from the human resources department.

Second, all interviewers should know why a candidate is being interviewed. Distribution of the Profile would provide this information.

Third, candidates should be escorted and introduced to the next interviewer by the previous interviewer. If there were any unavoidable interruptions in the schedule, the candidate should not be left alone for any period of time.

Fourth, the hiring executive should spend time discussing

the position with the candidate, so that he/she knows, at least in general terms, the position's performance expectations.

Fifth, someone, most likely the hiring executive, should ensure that the candidate knows what to expect next, in terms of timing and action.

The flow of events on the interview day is only part of the overall selling of a candidate. But why should you be so concerned about selling the candidate on your company? There are several major reasons:

1. The obvious: You may want to hire the candidate.
2. The candidate may be a customer or may be in a position to recommend prospective customers to your company.
3. The candidate may be able to refer other candidates to your company.
4. You want all candidates, even those to whom you do not make an offer, to feel that this was one of the best companies they have visited and that they would be receptive to being considered for another position at a later date.

Selling the candidates on your company means that they should perceive your company in a positive light. Important factors include the company's current or potential position within the industry; the compatibility of its management style and "chemistry" to the candidate; and the duties of the position offered relative to each candidate's experience, capability, and interest. There is a fourth dimension, too. In addition to selling the candidates on your company, you must also consider selling them on the community and overall environment, too, especially where the situation calls for a candidate to relocate.

None of the above is meant to imply that you would or should present a false image to the candidate. In situations where a company misrepresents itself in one or more areas, the candidate who is hired often becomes disenchanted. If management is not honest with a candidate, the situation could develop into a major problem. Perhaps it is better to play down some of your "positives"; let the candidate discover them. At the same time, be forthright in describing any negatives.

Relocating Executives Requires Special Planning

Let's take the case of interviewing candidates for a top-level managerial position. Some candidates will come from outside your local geography and, thus, require relocation. The following list describes actions your company can take to attract candidates from outside your local area.

1. Make sure that travel arrangements for candidates to visit your company are complete and are communicated to the candidate. Provide the candidate with the home phone number of someone in your company, just in case.
2. Obviously, a traveler has more time constraints than a local candidate. Make sure all interviewers are aware of the candidate's interview schedule and that they adhere to it throughout the day.
3. You will want to interview your finalist candidate a second time. Invite his or her significant other to visit the area at the same time. You are going to need to sell that person on the community.
4. Arrange with a relocation firm to make a presentation on the area. Many business-oriented real estate firms will be very pleased to do this.
5. If the significant other is employed, determine if there are employers or employment services this person should look into during the visit.
6. Provide the candidate with a car and extra time and expenses to explore your community on his or her own.
7. Determine the candidate's current home market value, mortgage payments, and sales potential.
8. Have a financial plan in mind on how to handle major differences in housing costs if your candidate is moving from a low-cost area to one where costs are much higher. Companies that provide a mortgage differential payment treat it as a separate item from salary so as not to distort salary ranges.
9. Have a dinner with the candidate and significant other. This is an excellent time to find out if the significant other has any concerns about a relocation.

Making the Offer . . . Stick

You've found your ideal candidate—your winner. He will obviously be a fine addition to your company. How do you reel him in and land him? What is it going to take in terms of making an offer that he cannot refuse?

The value of your interview notes once again becomes obvious. At this stage, you need to go back and review them. If they are as good as they should be, you will have a record of the candidate's hot buttons. You know what things will attract him to a new job. You know what his compensation was, and you know what his future goals are. All of this information helps you to put together an attractive offer.

You are now ready to formulate the compensation package. A good rule of thumb is that if you are trying to persuade a candidate to leave a job and join you, you will probably discuss compensation in terms of an increase in salary of anywhere from 10 to 20 percent.

If the candidate is actively looking to change jobs, your compensation offer should range up to 10 percent higher than the current salary. If a candidate is out of work, a company would generally offer a starting salary similar to what he or she last earned.

It is important that the company not assume an adversarial position over the issue of compensation. You don't want the relationship to begin with a conflict.

One way of avoiding this is to test the offer before making a commitment. This can be done in a number of ways, but generally you can begin by telling the candidate that you want him or her to join your firm. Ask what kind of compensation would be fair. In most cases, you will get a good ballpark figure of what the candidate finds acceptable. Usually, a person who is excited about a position will be honest about the whole matter of compensation.

If you are using a third party such as a recruiting firm, have them present the offer in a way that doesn't commit the company. For example, you may have your recruiter say to the candidate, "Well, I think they are going to offer you compensation of around $65,000 to $75,000. Does that fit in with your thinking?''

The candidate may come back and say, "Well, I was thinking more around the low eighties.'' The recruiter, knowing what the offer might be, could then say, "Perhaps they can come a little closer to your requirements.'' Or, "That may be a little higher than they are thinking to start with. Would you consider something more within their range?''

By doing this, you can begin your negotiations with a candidate on a point of agreement rather than a point of disagreement.

It's not always a matter of compensation, however. You must also look at the hot buttons. What are the things the candidate liked about the job? What did he or she dislike? How important is a title to the candidate? Is it as important as compensation?

You should have discovered this during the interview. Sometimes people will take a title over compensation. A person who has never been a vice-president might consider it very important to have that title. You may have picked up additional hot buttons when talking to the references. These are all items that enter into your final offer.

Bonuses play an important part, too. If you have a bonus structure, give the candidate a range of what you think the bonus could be if everything works out as planned. Some companies offer stock options. Some employees prefer them, while others prefer cash bonuses.

Benefits programs can also play an important role, more for the lower- to middle-level employee than for the high-level executive. Some people take a job because they want to relocate to a new area. It could be an important factor to them and could make up for a little less compensation. Once again, by now you should know how the candidate feels about these things.

Job satisfaction ranks high among the things people want in a job, according to national surveys. If you take an individual out of a company less exciting than yours and offer a position that involves increased challenges and greater long-term rewards, the candidate should have good reasons to accept your offer.

In a recent situation where an individual was just anxious to leave his present company, compensation was not the all-important factor. It was much more important to him that he find the right situation, one that was both challenging and pleasurable. He finally accepted an offer 12 percent less than he was making. But he figured he would quickly reach his old salary and beyond because of the excitement and opportunity in the new job. Compensation is not the only factor that lands the candidate.

You have a winner in the water. If you have done your work properly and have the resources and environment available to meet the candidate's expectations, you should be able to make an offer good enough to land your new employee.

An Offer for George Spencer

Executives of the Alpha Corporation had spoken with a dozen different references and received very positive information. The college confirmed that George did receive the degree as he stated. The selection committee (vice-president for sales, Eastern regional sales manager, and the president) all compared their Candidate Evaluation Forms on George and the other finalist candidate. The final choice, made by the vice-president, was to pursue George. He would be a valuable addition to their management team.

In deciding what to offer, the vice-president reviewed his interview notes reflecting George's current status and hot buttons.

1. Last year he earned $85,000 ($65K salary; $20K bonus).
2. He received a car allowance of $450/month.
3. He likes Alpha because it is a young, fast-growing company.
4. The position would be a "ground-floor opportunity."
5. He wants to be a "big fish in a little pond."
6. He understands a "lean and mean" environment.

7. His current, larger employer has a more substantial benefits package.
8. The vice-president had tested an offer to George
   by saying, "We probably won't offer you much
   more cash compensation than you're currently
   earning, but we can provide some different
   forms of incentives." Without requesting any
   details, George had responded favorably to that
   statement. He had previously mentioned during
   the interview that equity would be attractive, as
   Alpha was still a privately held company.

After conferring with the president, the vice-president
extended the following offer to George.

1. A base salary of $6,250.00 per month ($75,000
   annually). (He was told not to extend a formal
   salary offer in annual terms, as this could imply
   a contract for one year.)
2. A bonus based upon George's meeting his performance expectations *and* Alpha's profits for
   the year. This bonus could be up to 50 percent
   of his annual base salary.
3. A car allowance of $450 per month.
4. A stock option plan, with one-third vesting at
   the end of each year.
5. Benefits comparable to the other managers of
   Alpha.

George was excited about the opportunity to join Alpha.
He had given it considerable thought during the interview
process and the ensuing week. He was ready to accept and
did so on the spot. Alpha had figured out what it would take
to land him.

Throwing 'Em Back

After your offer has been accepted by the winning candidate,
you have other candidates who need to be informed that some-

one else has been hired for the position. It's important to close the loop with all candidates. It is just good business practice to demonstrate courtesy and to leave everyone with a good feeling about your company.

There are two ways to contact candidates. Those you have interviewed extensively deserve a personal telephone call. More than likely, these candidates are all winners, valuable individuals who may yet prove to be of value to you in some manner, somewhere down the line.

You should tell all these people that they were the top candidates, that you thought they were great, but that someone else had a little more appropriate experience than they did. Tell the candidates that you would like to keep them in mind for future consideration. If you're really sincere, ask them to keep in touch so you can track their careers. Thank all the candidates for the time they have spent with you, say how unfortunate it is that there is only one position open, and wish them luck.

As for the candidates with whom you did not spend much time, write or telephone, depending upon the situation. Essentially, you can say the same thing as above, if you genuinely feel that a candidate deserves special consideration. I am not encouraging hypocrisy here, merely courtesy.

It is important to let all the candidates know as soon as you have made a decision. There is nothing worse for a candidate than waiting to hear the verdict past a reasonable length of time—don't let it go longer than a week to ten days after your new hire has agreed to join the company.

As noted earlier, every one of these candidates could become a candidate again sometime in the future. Some of them might refer other people to your company or become customers themselves one day. For these reasons alone all candidates are worthy of good treatment from you.

You have now closed the loop. From defining your need to landing your winner, you have gone through all the vital steps in the PIE Selection System.

Thus far, I have tried to explain and illustrate the theoretical workings of the PIE System. But theory is only theory. How can the PIE System be applied to your particular hiring needs? How could it be established in your company as a practical, working system, training your people and ensuring that they use it? Who will make it happen?

The next chapter will show you how to make the PIE your own.

17

Making Your Own PIE

Theory is a wonderful thing. There are people who deeply appreciate each new theory they discover and who enjoy discussing theories at cocktail parties and other gatherings. Unfortunately, many of these people don't practice these theories and simply move on to the next brilliant new idea.

You now have the theory of the PIE Candidate Selection System. It is not complex, and it is workable. But it works only if used. Your next step is to put the system to use in your company or business. There is no better time to start than now.

Start Now!

The reasons you should start now are obvious: You will have immediate improvement in your selection process, and you will minimize risk in the hiring of your next professionals.

But the application of any new theory takes a significant amount of education, particularly in a large company. People need to think in a new way so that they begin to consider hiring in terms of results. For one thing, job descriptions should not be used as hiring criteria. Instead, by using performance expectations you can now define your needs in terms of real results. Starting now, you should also begin to improve your network of contacts, your system of retrieving contacts, and your sourcing of new candidates.

Your best incentive to start now is that poor hiring practices

pose many immediate and ongoing dangers. It is fairly common
today for companies who hire new people at any level to give
them enough rope to hang themselves, so to speak. It may have
taken you three months on average to find new employees, but
it could be another three months before you know if they will
succeed. An executive who plays a significant role in your
company could make a plethora of bad and ultimately costly
decisions during that time.

If the hire does not work out, you have a problem. You
either have to terminate the person or change his or her position
within the company. In either case, you have to start all over
again to find a new person. Adding it up, you can lose virtually
a full year of opportunity and profits and in its place endure a
year of unnecessary expenses. Add to this the lingering effects
that hiring mistakes have upon company morale. Bad hiring is
just bad for the company. It loses money, momentum, energy,
and time.

The PIE System is designed to prevent this from occurring.
Implementing this system cannot happen soon enough!

Your PIE Ally

Companies fortunate to have a strong, professional human resources person or department will have an ally in the implementation of the PIE process. In fact, the human resources department, and I will refer to it as HR department although it may
only be one person, should be the focal point of the PIE process.
(Should the company not have an HR professional, then a key
executive will need to initiate and maintain the process.)

The HR department can and should make a major contribution to the selection of winners. HR activities that would
enhance the effectiveness of implementing the PIE System include the following:

1. Training: Helping managers and supervisors in the development of the Profile and the improvement of their
   interviewing skills
2. Sourcing: Establishing a skills bank of current employ-

ees and a source bank of prospective candidates and
serving as a clearinghouse for all names gathered

3. Interviewing: Adding another dimension by providing input to hiring supervisors on candidates being
   considered?
4. Reference checking
5. Directing and coordinating specific recruitment projects
6. Identifying and monitoring the factors that make up the
   "chemistry" of the corporation
7. Developing the various ongoing recruiting programs,
   such as college recruiting, hiring bonus programs, etc.
8. Establishing and administering the corporate relocation
   program
9. Obtaining the names of prospective candidates during
   the employee orientation
10. Providing interviewing guidelines on questions that may
    and may not be asked to ensure compliance with EEO
    and other legislation
11. Establishing compensation programs and ranges, to
    ensure that the company is competitive in its offerings

There are some executives who tend to do their *own* recruiting, excluding the involvement of the HR department. If the
corporation has a professional HR department, these executives
are missing out on a valuable resource.

Educating Your Team

A number of natural laws can upset even the most carefully
prepared plans. One of these is the well-known Murphy's Law.
Another is the law of inertia, which states that a body prefers to
remain at rest rather than enter a state of motion. It is one of the
prime reasons why good plans fail. Nothing happens unless
something or somebody makes it happen.

The first step in implementing the PIE System is to assign
someone to be the PIE leader within the company. This person
will be responsible for the implementation and practice of the
PIE System. Without such a person in charge, the system is
likely to remain theoretical.

If the company is large enough to have a human resources department, as we discussed, that is the logical place to find the PIE leader. In small companies that don't have this luxury, the president or someone in a significant executive position should take on the leadership role to introduce the PIE program.

The next step is to have the relevant people involved in all aspects of hiring learn the steps explained here with the purpose of gaining an overall understanding of what the PIE System is all about. Relevant people include not only those responsible for hiring employees but also all supervisors and anyone who aspires to be a supervisor/manager. (Even if that promotion may not occur for a year or two, this is the best time to get them involved in the program.)

The PIE System is best implemented as a group effort. It's a good idea to establish workshops where employees can start practicing the PIE steps, beginning with the creation of Profiles.

As an example, the managers in the engineering department could get together to develop a Profile for some position that they either have to fill now or expect to open up in the future. Or the company president could take the lead and develop a Profile for one of the management positions immediately below him on the organization chart.

It is likely that developing the first Profiles will involve a number of attempts. Here is another reason why it is best to conduct this as a group effort. Different people will gain different insights, but if they attack development of the first Profiles as a group, a well-rounded and complete picture will emerge through their joint efforts.

Interviewing Workshops

Once you have fully developed the first Profiles, the next step in the introduction of the PIE System is to develop the team's interviewing skills. This should also be done in a workshop format. (See the Appendix, Conducting a PIE Workshop.)

It bears repeating yet again that interviewing is a skill that can be learned with practice.

We have shown you how to conduct the interview using

many of the tools available and how to set the agenda the interview should follow. We have even included the kinds of questions you can ask. But none of these tools and techniques are worth much unless you practice how to use them.

There are a number of ways to set up the workshops, depending upon the size of the group. A particularly effective method is to have one person be the interviewer and one person be the candidate, with the rest of the group as observers. Everyone should work from the same Profile.

The interview must be done with a Profile in mind. All prospective interviewers must learn to consult the Profile. They must realize that the Profile's success patterns and personal characteristics delineate the information they need to discover. After all, looking for these assets is the primary purpose of all interviewing.

The interviewer's job is to:

- Practice what you have read.
- Use the proper type of questions and the prompts.
- Find and identify success patterns and personal characteristics.

The candidate's job is to:

- Be yourself.
- Assume you do not know the interviewer.
- Volunteer what you want to reveal.
- Relax, have fun.

The observer's job is to:

- Note examples of good interviewing techniques, such as the types of questions and prompts.
- Make a list of the success patterns and personal characteristics uncovered during the interview.
- Note where you would have probed further on a particular issue, or any way you would have handled the interview differently.

When the interview has been completed, the PIE leader can open a discussion to analyze what went on. The leader should ensure that the criticism is not malicious and is only constructive. People are developing a new skill and need encouragement in order to succeed.

Another possibility is to use a video camera to film each interview and then replay the tape during the discussion. This gives the interviewers the opportunity not only to hear the critique but to see themselves in action. Afterward, in the same session or later sessions, others can take turns playing the different roles.

These interviewing sessions have to be constantly repeated in order for your people to hone their skills. Be sure that each person gets to play each role so that everyone gets practice. After a few sessions, you will note that the confidence and ability of participants have greatly improved.

Starting at the Top

Many people resist change. It is comfortable for them to continue what they are doing. The key to bring about change in your company, particularly in this area of selection, is to start from the top.

Someone high in the company, the chief executive, the president, has to say, "From now on, this is the way it is going to be done. This is going to have an impact on the company. It is going to improve our methods of hiring and selecting people. It will minimize our risks, and we are going to start right now."

Part of this leader's function is to insist that any new hire or transfer within the company will not be approved unless the request has a Profile attached to it. This automatically gets the process started and forces the departmental heads and others to formulate their requirements and desires.

Use of the PIE System should become firm company policy. There will always be reasons and excuses not to do it—an emergency situation, a vital need, not enough time, an ideal person immediately available—but the company head must ignore this kind of evasion. His or her answer to this should be:

"Let me see the Profile." The staff will soon realize that this is the only acceptable method to fill positions.

A time-tested teaching method has always been through example. Therefore, if the president of the company needs to hire someone, he or she should go through the process of developing a Profile for that position.

Even in the face of time and other pressures, the president should not allow someone else to develop the Profile. The person who holds the reins of power should know better than anyone else what results need to be achieved by the company's managers. Any evasion of this responsibility will send a clear message to employees that the system is unimportant.

Insistence upon this policy is an effective way to control managers to ensure that when they say they need someone, they know what the results they must achieve and what kind of person they need. The PIE System is a very effective cost and efficiency control mechanism. It also forces managers to look internally to see if there is anyone in the company who can achieve those results, thus eliminating the need for an additional hire.

Not only is the Profile important in terms of hiring new people, but it is also a good disciplinary procedure to ensure that the needs are real and that the means to fill those needs do not already exist.

The Real Thing

Particularly in the beginning stages of implementing the PIE System, after the first real interviews have been conducted, it is a good idea to bring together all the people who have interviewed the candidates. Several staff members will have interviewed the same candidate, filled out Candidate Evaluation Forms, and turned the forms into the PIE leader.

At this meeting, all the interviewers should have the opportunity to tell how they found out information, why they evaluated the candidate in the way they did, what they found out, and where they need more information.

It is then the job of the PIE leader, who should have an

overview of the whole process, to point out any discrepancies so that they can be reconciled. It will be an amazing process, I guarantee. As the team members start to talk among themselves, consulting their notes, they will discover that "So-and-so asked this kind of question and got that information, but so-and-so didn't think about that." Everyone can learn and improve.

This kind of on-the-job learning is the most effective of all. You can go through all kinds of workshops and practice sessions, but actually conducting a real interview of a real candidate will teach more about interviewing in a shorter period of time than anything else.

However, after the first real interviews, the managers could get together for another workshop, this time utilizing everything they have learned. It is necessary to continue reinforcing what you are learning before it can become second nature.

Quality Control

The implementation of any new system faces an uphill battle, and the PIE Selection System is no exception. The first step is to get the system used, and the second step is to get it used properly. For any number of reasons—laziness, ineptitude, creativity, and more—people have an impulse to change a system so that it will fit into their own thinking.

The PIE System is designed in the way it is because it works. While some adaptation is permissible—there are, after all, differences among companies—none of the basic steps should be left out. You must make sure not to let anything slip and particularly to see that the company does not hire anyone who has not gone through the entire Profile, Interview, Evaluate process.

The best quality-control tool we have developed happens also to be very simple. It is a checklist that everyone involved in a new hire is required to utilize. It will show if the Profile was done, if all methods of sourcing were taken into consideration, if everyone turned in a Candidate Evaluation Form, and if the references were checked.

The checklist in Figure 4 is fairly generic and can be utilized

Figure 4. PIE System Checklist.

Answer each of the following questions to ensure that every step of the system has been completed.

CONTROL

_____ Have we assigned a recruiting project leader?

PROFILE DEVELOPMENT

_____ Were the performance expectations based on realistic and expected results?
_____ Do success patterns reflect experiences and skills that should lead to the accomplishments of these results?
_____ Are the personal characteristics representative of both the company's style and the results desired?

SOURCING

_____ Does the Profile suggest that we really need to hire an addition to the company, or
_____ Have we considered current employees for this position, utilizing our skills bank?
_____ Have we alerted all employees about this requirement, so they might recommend candidates?
_____ Have we thoroughly reviewed our source bank of prospects, including résumés and applications, business card files, and referrals from hires?
_____ Do we need to advertise this position? Where?
_____ Should we seek assistance from a recruiting firm?
_____ Have we reviewed all the sources in _Hiring Winners_?

INTERVIEWING

_____ Have we reviewed the résumés or applications for areas that pose questions (the yellow flags)?
_____ Do all interviewers have a copy of the Profile?
_____ Do all interviewers have Candidate Evaluation Forms?
_____ Have all interviewers been trained in interviewing, and in evaluating the candidates?
_____ Have we determined all candidates' hot buttons?
_____ After the interviews, have all the evaluation forms been completed and turned in?

(continues)

Figure 4. (*Continued.*)

EVALUATION

_____ Have we checked references with peers, subordinates, and superiors?

_____ Have we checked references with people beyond the names supplied by the candidate?

_____ Have we verified academic credentials?

_____ Have we compared candidates to the Profile?

_____ Have we compared candidates to each other?

OFFER

_____ Do we know what it will take to hire the candidate?

_____ Have we "tested" the offer before it is formally presented?

CLOSING

_____ Have we informed all candidates of our decision?

_____ Have we placed nonhired candidates in our source bank?

---

by any kind of company. It covers all the steps in the PIE Selection System and makes sure they have all been covered in the search for a winner.

This Checklist is a tool that should be utilized as a standard by those responsible for hiring. If several people are involved in the hire, the PIE leader should be the one to refer to the list, checking off each action as it is done and thus ensuring that no steps are missed.

If use of this list becomes firm company policy, nothing will be overlooked in the hiring process. Assuming that all the steps have been followed fully and correctly, the result will be a winning hire.

The Pendulum Swings

Once upon a time, employers could hire anyone they wished to hire, thoroughly controlling the total interview and selection process. If they wished, they were able to discriminate against racial and ethnic minorities, against a person with different religious and lifestyle preferences, and against women and people over forty. If a manager chose to fire someone, he could do it at will and for any reason.

Many employment candidates were naïve, easily intimidated prey, seeking to make a good impression in order to obtain and hold a job. Generally poor writing skills produced equally poor résumés. Interrogatory interviews brought something like mental anguish.

Gradually, all this has changed. Federal and state laws have made it much more difficult to discriminate on the hiring side, and increased civil litigation has attacked unlawful terminations.

Many candidates have been educated in the hiring process. Today, with the help of professionals, they are skillfully "marketed" to employers. Professional résumé writers can make anyone look good. Courses on image and dress and how to present oneself during the job interview can make candidates look even better. And books, books, and more books have provided job seekers with everything they need to know but were afraid to ask about landing *the* job. Even corporations help, preparing "terminated" employees to search for a new job through outplacement services.

Many employers today are virtually defenseless against this swing of the pendulum. Candidates have become more than a match for their hiring counterparts. Employers never learned in college how to select employees, and no books provide an easy system to help the employer get back in control. Today, in many cases, it is the candidate who intimidates and controls the interview.

I am not suggesting that federal and state laws were unwarranted. On the contrary, they have forced employers to make decisions based upon the real skills of candidates. And where these skills were the ones truly required, such laws have made for a more productive work force.

Today, employers not only need to comply with these laws, but they also have to hone their selection capabilities. And it is to deal with this issue that the PIE Selection System was developed.

If you apply the system properly, I guarantee that you will see immediate improvement in your hiring practices. Whether your company is large or small, whether it hires a dozen people or a thousand, application of the PIE System will help you lessen your risks and find the winners that you need. Good hunting!

Appendix

Conducting a
PIE Workshop

The material presented in this appendix will assist you in implementing the PIE Selection System. It is offered as a guide; experience will help you determine how to tailor the workshop to meet your particular requirements.

As these are practice sessions to establish and/or improve selection skills, the workshop should be exactly that—a workshop, not a lecture. Consequently, all participants should have read the book and have some understanding of the PIE process of selecting winners.

The workbook pages shown should be reprinted on 8½- by 11-inch paper to be used in the workshop.

How to Make the Workshop Most Effective

1. *Common Denominator:* It is best to select a single recruitment requirement with which all of the participants have some familiarity. As examples, titles such as salesperson, production supervisor, or perhaps accounting manager might be used. Most of the people in the workshop should be able to visualize the position and to project the results to be achieved by this person in the company. Someone from "that person's" department will be in the group, and can provide the reality to the exercises.

2. *Suggested Format and Timetable:* Following is an outline of how to structure a two-day workshop.

Session	Topics and Tasks	Allotted Hours
	Day One	
1.	Developing a Profile	2–3
A.	Defining performance expectations	1
B.	Identifying success patterns	0.5
C.	Identifying personal characteristics	0.5
D.	Identifying the absolutes	0.25
2.	Sourcing for Candidates and Résumé Review	1–2
A.	Developing a source list	1
B.	Identifying "flags" in a résumé	1
	Day Two	
3.	Interviewing Candidates	0.5*
4.	Evaluating Candidates	
A.	Discussing Candidate Evaluation Form	0.5
B.	Developing reference questions	0.5

*Per Participant

3. *Leader:* Designated PIE implementing executive, who serves as facilitator/trainer for the workshop.

4. *Participants:* Six to twelve managers/professionals.

5. *Setting:* Private conference or meeting room set up in classroom style or U shape. Small table in front, with two chairs.

6. *Materials:* One to two easels and flip charts, markers, and masking tape. A set of forms as shown at the end of this appendix.

First Session: Developing a Profile

Task A. Defining Performance Expectations

Directions: Participants decide on a "common denominator" position. Participants are instructed to "consider the results you would expect the successful candidate to have achieved if he or she had been in that position for one year. Be specific. Quantify and define these results in objective, measurable terms." All participants should take the first fifteen minutes to develop their own lists of performance expectations using Form 1. From the individual lists a common list of performance expectations can be compiled and written on the flip charts. (These charts should be placed on the walls for referral throughout all sessions.)

Task B. Identifying Success Patterns

Directions: Using the agreed-upon list of performance expectations, participants are instructed to "develop a list of success patterns—specific experiences, skills, and accomplishments you feel candidates should or must have in their background to be able to achieve the desired results." The participants should take five to ten minutes to make their own lists, using Form 2, and then a mutual list will be developed by the group. Again, these should be displayed for everyone to refer to later.

Task C. Identifying Personal Characteristics

Directions: There are two parts to this exercise: first, to develop a list of performance characteristics specific to the position; second, to develop a list of "generic" attributes that should be common to any professional joining the company. With the second part, the more workshops you conduct, the more you will be able to identify the "chemistry" of people who will work best on the company's team and in its particular environment.

Instructions to participants should include the following: "Using Form 3, develop a list of personal characteristics—personality traits and workstyle patterns that you believe candidates must have in order to achieve the performance expectations. Additionally, come up with a list of characteristics that you believe to be important in achieving success in our company." Develop a group composite list and tape this up on the walls where all can see it.

Task D. Identifying the Absolutes

Directions: Participants are to decide which success patterns and which personal characteristics are absolutes—the attributes that a candidate must have to be considered for the position. These absolutes should be marked with an asterisk on the composite sheets. It should be emphasized that while Absolutes are significant in the selection process, too many will result in eliminating most, if not all candidates.

Prior to the third session, the leader should create a Candidate Evaluation Form based on the composite lists and absolutes defined in the first session.

Second Session: Sourcing for Candidates and Résumé Review

Task A. Developing a Source List

Directions: Considering the success patterns and personal characteristics, the group works together to develop a comprehensive list of sources for finding candidates. This should be a brainstorming session with no holds barred, although specifics are important. For example, do not say, "we should talk to our customers." Rather, the customers need to be identified along with the contact within the customer business.

All approaches should be utilized. The sources listed in Chapter 6 should be reviewed to determine which might apply to this particular situation.

Depending on the position under consideration, the leader should not be satisfied with less than 25 to 50 viable sources. This list should be printed on flip charts.

Task B. Identifying "Flags" in a Résumé

Directions: Participants will review two résumés and complete Form 4 for each.

The leader selects two résumés that have been submitted to

the company (names should be blocked out before distributing to the participants). These résumés should each be at least two pages in length and should be typical of the résumés usually received. Select résumés that depict candidates at the career level of the participants.

Third Session: Interviewing Candidates

The purpose of this session is for the participants to develop interviewing skills through practice, observation, and constructive criticism. Each interview session is followed by a critique by the observers and the candidate.

This is a role-playing session. One participant is the candidate, one is the interviewer, and everyone else is an active observer. Each person will get a turn as candidate and interviewer.

Interviewer's Role: To interview the candidate, using question styles, probes, body language, and every other technique discussed in the book. The goal, as in any interview, is to discover the success patterns and personal characteristics of the candidate.

Candidate's Role: There are two role options for the candidate. (1) Be yourself, and reveal anything you would like to reveal. It would be most logical for each participant to be considered for a job something like the one he or she actually holds. (2) Act as a candidate for the position developed in the Profile. This is more difficult because you need to develop the part as you get into the interview. Either role will provide good practice for the interviewer and the observers.

Observer's Role: To note and comment on good interviewing techniques used by the interviewer. To list the success patterns and personal characteristics uncovered. To note where and how you would have probed further, or how you would have handled the interview differently. Observers should complete Form 5 for each interview.

Leader's Role: To facilitate the rotation of assignments approximately every twenty to thirty minutes. To facilitate the critique and discussion after each interview. The following points should be brought out during the critique.

1. How did the interviewer feel during the interview?
2. How did the candidate feel during the interview?
3. Review the observers' comments from *Form 5*.

Fourth Session: Evaluating Candidates

Task A. Discussing Candidate Evaluation Form

Leader distributes Candidate Evaluation Form developed from the example in the second session. Discussion focuses on:

1. When and how to complete the form, including how to use the Completely, Moderately, and Doubtful measures
2. The process of evaluating candidates (a) against the Profile, (b) by several interviewers, (c) against each other.

Task B. Developing Reference Questions

Directions: Refer back to the résumés that were critiqued in the second session. Each participant should complete the information requested on Form 6. The group then should discuss these answers.

Form 1   Defining Performance Expectations

Position Title_____

Performance expectations: The results we want to accomplish by having someone in the position, defined in specific, measurable terms. These results are to be completed within one year or less. (Define the number of months in which the result should be completed.)

1.

2.

3.

4.

5.

6.

7.

8.

9.

10.

Form 2   *Identifying Success Patterns*

Position Title_____

Success patterns: Specific experiences, skills, and accomplishments candidates should have in their backgrounds to be able to achieve the performance expectations. These success patterns should be measurable and verifiable.

1.

2.

3.

4.

5.

6.

7.

8.

9.

10.

11.

12.

13.

Form 3   *Identifying Personal Characteristics*

Position Title_____

Personal Characteristics: Personality traits and workstyle patterns that candidates should have to meet the performance expectations.

1.	7.
2.	8.
3.	9.
4.	10.
5.	11.
6.	12.

The company's "generic" personal characteristics:

1.	7.
2.	8.
3.	9.
4.	10.
5.	11.
6.	12.

Form 4   Identifying "Flags" in a Résumé

Review the résumé carefully, then answer the following questions:

1. What is the position for which this person is applying?

2. Is that position a logical career progression? And why, or why not?

3. List the "yellow flags" you have uncovered. Consider unaccountable time gaps, short-term job patterns, positions described in generalities rather than accomplishments, or others.

4. What three specific questions would you like to ask of this candidate?

5. Can you make any assumptions about this person's personal characteristics and how they might fit in with your team's "chemistry"?

Form 5　　　*Interview Observations*

1. Note examples of both positive and negative techniques used by the interviewer.

2. List the success patterns and personal characteristics uncovered.

3. Note where, why, and how you would have probed further on any particular issue, and how you would have handled the interview differently.

Form 6   *Developing Reference Questions*

A. Create a question to clarify or verify some perceived success pattern or personal characteristic that was generated by information on the résumé. Provide one question for each résumé. Indicate to whom would you address your question.

B. Develop a list of at least five questions you would ask about *all* candidates when checking references.

   1.

   2.

   3.

   4.

   5.

Index

Italic page references refer to figures.

177

results
  definition of job in terms of, 14–15
  in-depth analysis of, 13
  and performance expectations, 22–24
résumés
  flags in, 74–75
  identification of flags in, 174
  sample of, 76, 77–79
  in source bank, 48–49

selection process
  activities in, 4–5
  location of candidates in, 43–50
  poorly handled, 143–144
  proper handling of, 144–145
  vital steps in, 2–4
  see also hiring; PIE Selection System
seminars, candidates from, 62–63
skills bank
  location of candidates through, 44
  recruiting from, 47–50
source bank
  development of, 48
  recruiting from, 47–50
  synthesis of information in, 49–50

stress interview theory, 89
success patterns, 14, 28–31
  absolutes in, 35–38, 41
  elements of, 28
  evaluation of, 123
  form to identify, 172
  sample of, 41
  tracking, in interview, 84–85, 87–88
summer employees, as source of candidates, 63

teachers, as source of candidates, 59
temporary employment agencies, 63–64
time
  cost of, 4–6
  lack of, 9–10
trade association directories, 56
trade shows, as source of candidates, 64

winners
  blueprint for, 28–42
  how to find, 51–64
  personal characteristics of, 32
  reasons for hiring of, 1